GW's Ultimate Unofficial Guide MINECRAFT CONTENTS

4	A Year of Minecraft	42	Guide to the Trial Chambers
6	Minecraft Timeline	44	Guide to Trial Chamber Mobs
10	Guide to Starting Out	46	GamesWarrior Review: A Minecraft Movie
16	Biome Basics: The Overworld	48	Guide to Enchantments and Potions
20	Guide to the Pale Garden	52	Guide to the Nether
21	Mob Profile: Creaking	55	Mob Profile: Wither
22	Guide to Friendly Mobs	56	Villagers and Trading
26	Building Review: Sea Diary	60	Treasures of the Overworld
28	Crafting Recipes	66	Guide to Hostile Mobs
30	Recipes to Try!	70	Guide to The End
32	Guide to the Deep Dark	73	Mob Profile: The Ender Dragon
33	Mob Profile: Warden	74	Mega Minecraft Quiz
34	The Best Blocks	76	Puzzle and Quiz Answers
36	Building Step-by-Step: Ultimate Overworld Base		

Little Brother Books Ltd, 23 Southernhay East, Exeter, Devon, EX1 1QL

books@littlebrotherbooks.co.uk | www.littlebrotherbooks.co.uk

The Little Brother Books trademarks, logos, email, and website addresses are sole and exclusive properties of Little Brother Books Limited.

Published 2025. Printed in Italy.

Little Brother Books, 77 Camden Street Lower, Dublin D02 XE80.

This is an unofficial and independently written book, the inclusion of any logos, images, quotes and references does not imply endorsement. Whilst every care has been taken in researching and writing this book, due to the nature of the subject matter, some information may change over time.

Minecraft is a registered trademark of Mojang and Microsoft.

The screenshots and artwork shown in this guide were taken from Minecraft in-game screenshots, a game created and published by Mojang and Microsoft. This is a 100% unofficial and independent guide, which is in no way licensed, authorised or endorsed by, or otherwise connected in anyway with, Mojang and Microsoft or any other individuals from Mojang and Microsoft and authors of Minecraft.

All copyrights and trademarks are recognised and used specifically for the purpose of criticism, review and reportage.

Images used under license from Adobe Stock.

A YEAR OF MINECRAFT

It's been an amazing year for Mojang's massively popular video game, with plenty of exciting content drops, epic events and even an amazing live-action movie. Check out GamesWarrior's review of what's been happening over the last 12 months in the blocky world of Minecraft!

NEW DROP FEATURES

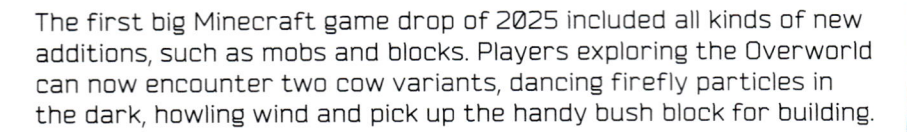

The first big Minecraft game drop of 2025 included all kinds of new additions, such as mobs and blocks. Players exploring the Overworld can now encounter two cow variants, dancing firefly particles in the dark, howling wind and pick up the handy bush block for building.

GamesWarrior VERDICT
These additions make the game even better!

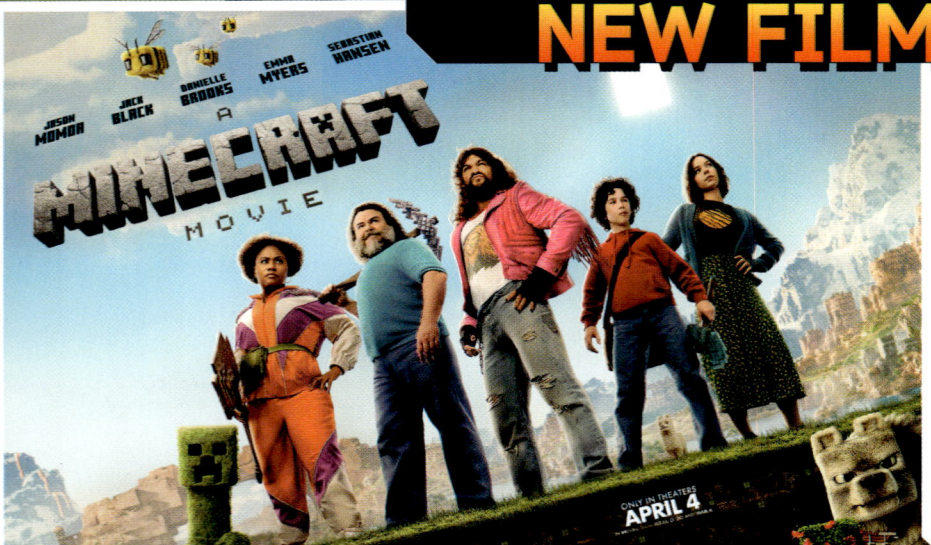

BLOCKBUSTING NEW FILM!

Arriving on big screens around the world on April 4, 2025 was *A Minecraft Movie*, starring Jack Black as Steve.

Alongside the film, Mojang also released A Minecraft Movie: Add-On, which included buck-chuckets, the Orb of Dominance, Piglin General and Great Hog.

GamesWarrior VERDICT
A Minecraft Movie is awesome!

THE PALE GARDEN

An all-new biome was added to Minecraft in 2024 – the creepy pale garden! It features a forest filled with white, pale oak trees and a sinister mob, the creaking.

You can find out how to beat the creaking in the guide on page 21..

GAMESWARRIOR VERDICT
This is one creepy mob!

MINECRAFT EXPERIENCE: VILLAGER RESCUE

From April 2025, fans could check out the Minecraft Experience: Villager Rescue in London. The immersive event allowed families to dive into the Overworld in person, as if you are in the actual game!

Complete the quest to receive a limited-edition half-zombie, half-villager cape to use in the game!

GAMESWARRIOR VERDICT
It's like being in Minecraft for real!

PLAYER LOCATOR BAR

The Player Locator bar lets friends find each other in a world. Players can still stay hidden though, by sneaking around, wearing a mask or drinking a potion of Invisibility.

GAMESWARRIOR VERDICT
This is one feature fans have been requesting for years.

UPDATED SPAWN EGGS

New spawn egg textures now come in three sizes. That means they look like the mobs that will emerge from them, making it easier to know what you're hatching in advance.

GAMESWARRIOR VERDICT
Some of the mob eggs look hilarious!

MINECRAFT LIVE

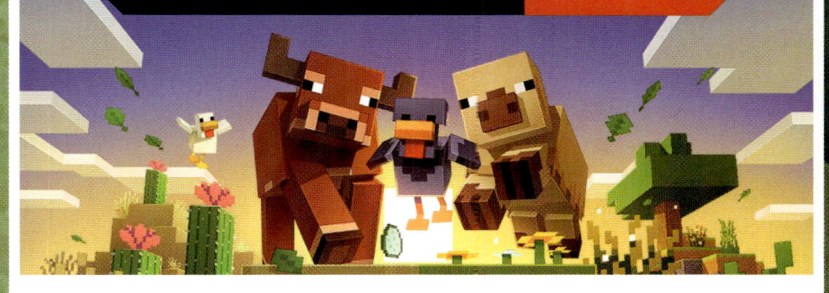

All sorts of new content was revealed at this year's Minecraft LIVE event. Fans were able to watch Mojang unveil surprises such as the Spring to Life update, the dried ghast block, ghastlings, happy ghasts and more!

GAMESWARRIOR VERDICT
There's all sorts of great stuff on the way soon!

MINECRAFT TIMELINE

Minecraft was released in 2009, with the game having been created by Markus 'Notch' Persson. Since then, the Mojang title has received multiple updates, spin-off games, physical merchandise and even a big screen movie – so let's dive into the key events over the years!

Markus 'Notch' Persson creates Minecraft, which is released as a public beta with Steve as the only mob. Original names considered were 'Cave Game' and 'The Order of the Stone'.

Full release of Minecraft on November 18, 2011. To celebrate, new additions include the End, endermen and the ender dragon. Minecraft: Pocket Edition arrives on mobile devices.

2009   2010   2011   2012

Mojang introduces the Pretty Scary update to Minecraft, including the chilling wither, plus the game gets a console version, landing on the Xbox 360. The first LEGO Minecraft sets release.

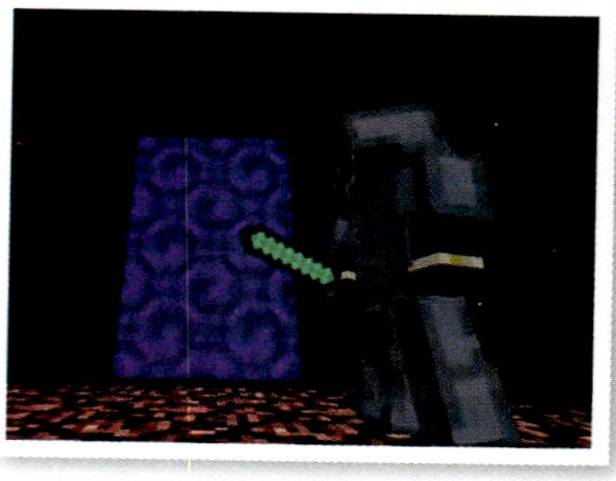

Survival Mode added to Minecraft, along with skeletons, zombies and the Nether, plus a crafting system is introduced. The first-ever MINECON takes place in Bellevue, USA!

Fans rejoice as horses are finally added to Minecraft! The Java Edition of Minecraft also receives a massive content drop in the shape of The Update that Changed the World.

Minecraft releases for the Nintendo Wii U, with Minecraft: Story Mode also available the same year, changing the way that players can interact with the game.

Terrestrial!

2013   2014   2015   2016

Microsoft buys Mojang for a whopping $2.5 billion! Minecraft launches on PlayStation 4 and Xbox One. The Bountiful Update adds new survival features and coarse dirt blocks.

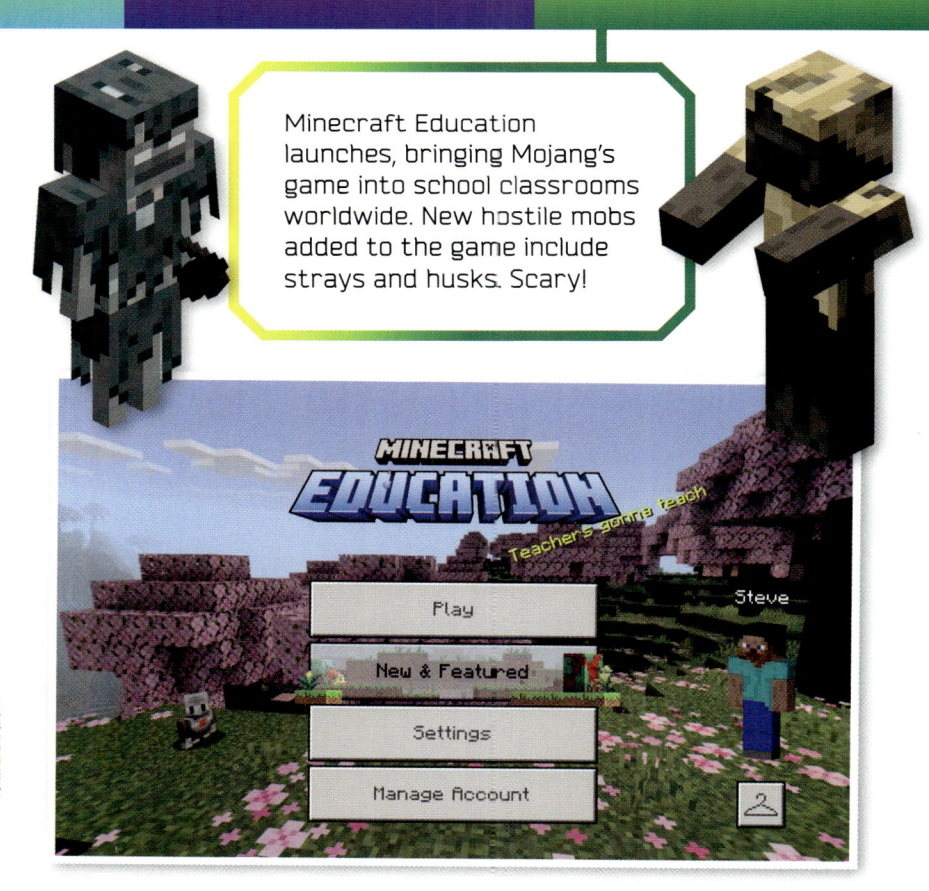

Minecraft Education launches, bringing Mojang's game into school classrooms worldwide. New hostile mobs added to the game include strays and husks. Scary!

Teacher's gonna teach

Minecraft releases on Nintendo Switch, with the Better Together update adding crossplay support. The first novel based on the video game also arrives with Minecraft: The Island.

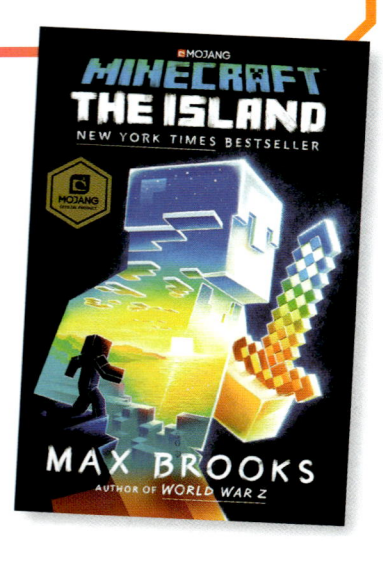

Mojang releases Minecraft Dungeons. This awesome spin-off title is a top-down dungeon crawler that's packed with characters and new mobs and ends up becoming a smash hit title!

2017   2018   2019   2020

Update Aquatic overhauls ocean biomes, adding turtles, pufferfish and dolphins, along with the phantom, a deadly flying mob voted for by fans of the game.

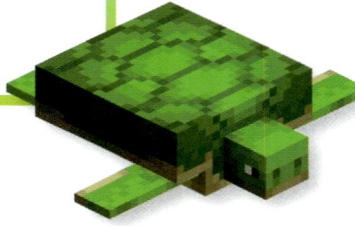

Minecraft celebrates its 10th anniversary in style! The Village and Pillage Update also launches, with lots of new blocks and mobs, along with the augmented reality game, Minecraft Earth.

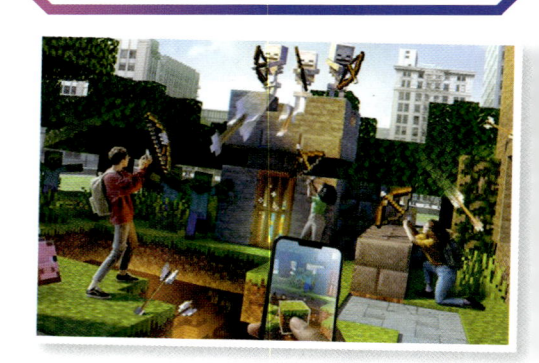

8

Two Caves & Cliffs updates arrive in the same year, bringing goats, axolotls and glow squid to the game. Plus, Minecraft Earth is officially shut down.

The live-action *A Minecraft Movie* releases on the big screen. Starring Jack Black and Jason Momoa, the film goes on to smash box office records and thrill fans all around the world!

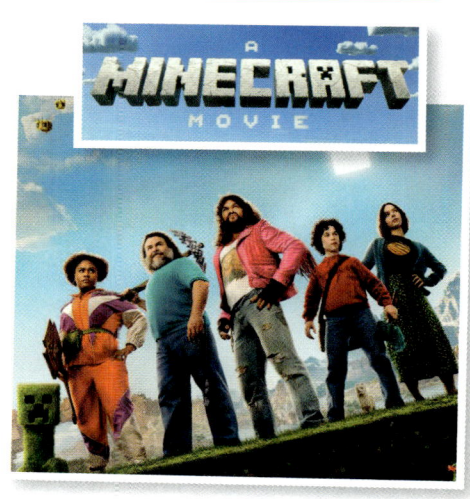

The Trails & Tales update brings archaeology to Minecraft, as well as camels and sniffers. Minecraft Legends is also released – a cross-platform real-time action-strategy title.

2021   2022   2023   2024   2025

Mangrove swamps, frogs and allays are added to the game, along with the spooky deep dark and the fearsome warden in The Wild Update.

Minecraft celebrates its 15th anniversary! The Tricky Trials update adds challenging trial chambers; the breeze, the mace, copper and tuff blocks, the crafter and the bogged.

GUIDE TO STARTING OUT

If you're just starting out on your Minecraft adventure, there are plenty of options available. GamesWarrior has taken a look at everything, from game modes, controller settings and avatar skins, to exploration strategies and weapons, so that you can jump right in!

CREATE AN ACCOUNT

To get started in Minecraft, you'll need to create a Microsoft child account. This will require an email address (either your own or an adult – with their approval), then you can create a cool Gamertag for your profile with a unique picture.

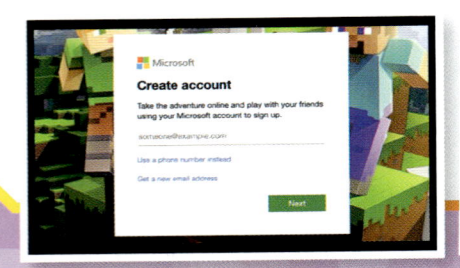

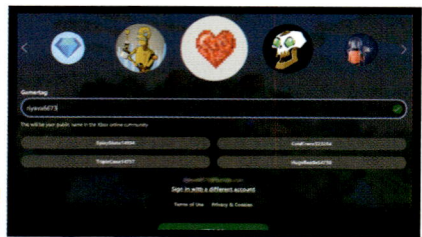

CONTROLLER SETTINGS

In you're playing Minecraft on a PC, you'll be using the mouse to look around, attack and use or place items, plus the keyboard for various commands. On consoles, players move about using the thumbstick, with actions assigned to controller buttons.

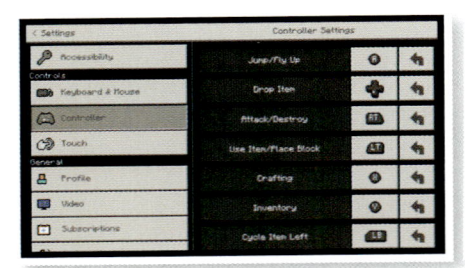

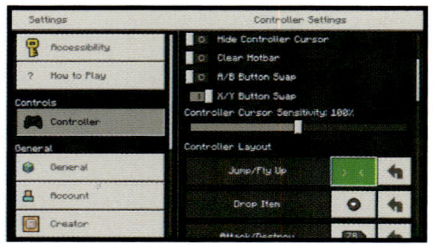

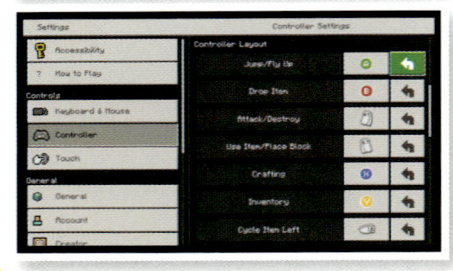

GAMESWARRIOR VERDICT

It may take you some time to get used to the controls or work out which settings are best for you, but once you do, you'll become an even better Minecraft player!

GAME MODES

Once you've downloaded Minecraft for free and logged in, you can decide which of the four game modes to try.

They include Survival, Creative, Adventure and Spectator, all of which have different rules for players to experience.

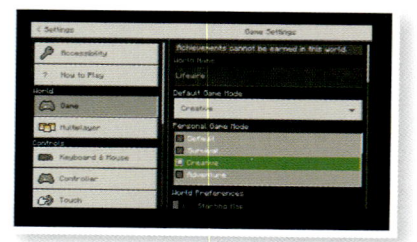

CHARACTERS

In Minecraft, players get to choose from one of nine default skins: Steve, Alex, Noor, Sunny, Ari, Zuri, Makena, Kai and Efe. Players can choose one of these characters and then customise how they'll look in the game.

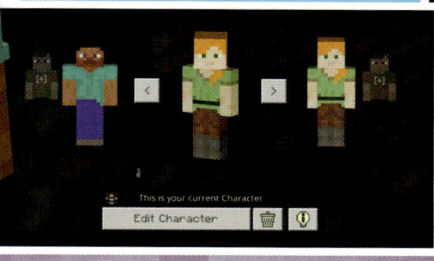

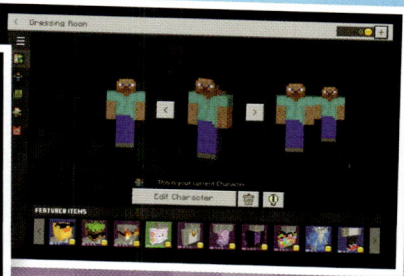

SKINS

Players are able to change the look of their character if they wish with skins available from the Minecraft Marketplace. Some skins are free, but others cost Minecoins, which can be purchased using real money.

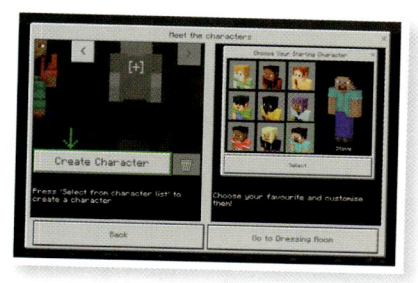

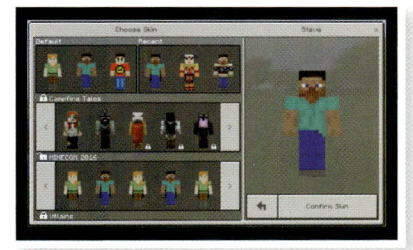

MARKETPLACE

The Minecraft Marketplace is packed with all kinds of goodies, including skin packs, worlds, adventure maps, mini-games, survival spawns, texture packs, add-ons and mash-up packs, all of which you may want to try at some point.

GAMESWARRIOR VERDICT

Buying items from the Minecraft Marketplace can add some cool stuff to your collection, but there's nothing more satisfying than grabbing lots of fun freebies!

11

EXPLORING

One of the main reasons Minecraft players enjoy the game so much, is because of the amount of exploring they can do. Most of your time will most likely be spent in the Overworld, a vast sprawling land that stretches as far as they eye can see.

BIOMES

Each Overworld level, or biome, is different from every other. Some offer flat, green plains and lush forests, while others feature chilling weather or scorching desert sands. Trying them all out is a good way to discover which you think is the best!

DIMENSIONS

As well as the Overworld, Minecraft offers other dimensions for more experienced gamers to tackle. They include the Nether and the End, two harsh realms that should only be tackled by real pros.

GAMESWARRIOR VERDICT

Spending lots of time in the Overworld can be very satisfying, but just wait and see what challenges the Nether and the End bring!

RESOURCES

The good news is that the Overworld has almost everything you will need to survive in the game. From food, water and shelter to resources for weapons, armour and tools – supplies are all around you.

GAMESWARRIOR VERDICT
Taking the time to fully explore exactly what the Overworld has to offer will help you become a much better Minecraft player over time!

MOBS

There are all kinds of different mobs to find in Minecraft, ranging from familiar animals to very strange creatures. Some will prove to be no threat at all and can sometimes be tamed, while others will attack you at every chance they get!

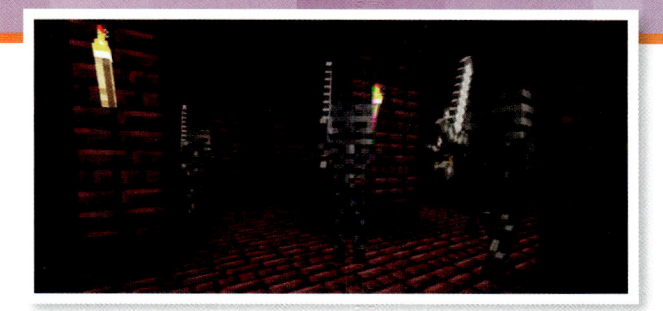

SURVIVING

Surviving in Minecraft can be a little tricky at first, but as time goes by you'll soon learn plenty of valuable skills. Those will include how to gather resources, mine, craft weapons, items and tools. Then how to battle hostile enemies, survive the night and access new dimensions!

NIGHT

The night is the most dangerous time in Minecraft. This is when many hostile mobs start to spawn, some of which will attack you on sight. You'll either have to avoid them altogether or battle them until the sun comes up.

BEDS

Once you've learned how to craft a bed, you'll find out just how handy they really are. Sleeping in a bed allows players to reset their spawn points and helps pass the night more quickly. But try sleeping in a bed in the Nether and it will explode!

TORCHES

If it's night or you're underground, be sure to carry a torch. These useful items can be crafted using the recipe shown and give off a light level of 14, which is plenty to illuminate the world all around you.

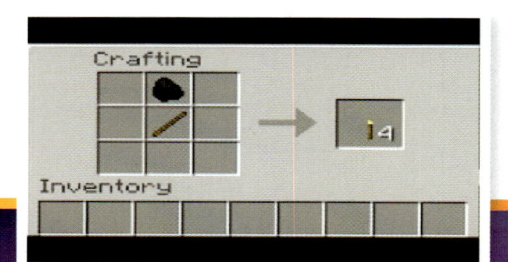

GAMESWARRIOR VERDICT

Torches are a simple and effective way of creating light in the dark and many players will carry lots of them when digging underground!

WEAPONS

Be sure to craft yourself a basic weapon as soon as you spawn into the Overworld. A simple wooden sword can be enough to defend yourself with, before you move on to making axes, bows, tridents and more.

TOOLS

Just as important in any game of Minecraft are tools, which are needed for performing some actions or doing them faster. Handy tools can include flint and steel, pickaxe, shovel, shears, hoe, fishing rod, brush, compass, spyglass and many others.

INVENTORY ITEMS

Any items that you find or craft during your adventures will be added to your inventory. From this screen, you can select items, craft new ones, equip tools and blocks, and view your character's skin.

GAMESWARRIOR VERDICT

With a fully stocked inventory, you should be ready to face any of the tough challenges that a game of Minecraft can throw at you!

BIOME BASICS
THE OVERWORLD

There are over 60 different biomes in some versions of Minecraft; worlds that have their own special features, weather, mobs and items. Here is GamesWarrior's lowdown on the different locations. By fully exploring these locations, players can boost their abilities, pick up all kinds of resources and beat the toughest of foes!

PLAINS

Plains were some of the first biomes added to Minecraft, flat grasslands that often border forests and savannas. Players may encounter villages on plains now and again, with tamed horses offering the best option for fast travel around the Overworld.

GAMESWARRIOR VERDICT
Plains are handy for finding flower blocks, but you won't last long without lots of resources.

SAVANNA

There are three different versions of this tall grass biome: savanna, savanna plateau and windswept savanna. These areas tend to be dry, with no rain or lightning. These are the only locations where acacia trees naturally generate.

GAMESWARRIOR VERDICT
A good biome for beginners to start off with, but the tall grass can obscure vision and make combat difficult.

JUNGLE

Jungle biomes are full of lush vegetation and can feature the tallest trees in the game! They tend to generate near forests and plains and are the exclusive home to parrots, ocelots and pandas.

GAMESWARRIOR VERDICT

It can be easy to get lost in dense jungle biomes, so drop a marker to guide you back to safety.

TAIGA

This grassland biome features lots of ferns and spruce, making it an ideal location for farming resources. Villages and trading posts can usually be found dotted around the location and be sure to keep an eye out for wolves, foxes, rabbits and other passive mobs too.

GAMESWARRIOR VERDICT

A great biome to start out in Survival mode, with all sorts of useful resources and friendly mobs waiting to be tamed.

SWAMPS

Swamp biomes can generate fossils, have rare underground structures in them and are where slimes and frogs spawn. As well as standard swamps, mangrove swamps can sometimes be encountered, which contain mangrove trees and seagrass.

GAMESWARRIOR VERDICT
These wetland biomes can be tricky to navigate, but stick with them and you'll find all sorts of useful items and blocks to collect.

CAVES

Usually located underground, caves can be great hiding places or bases but may also contain dangerous mobs! With the right tools, there are all kinds of ores and unique blocks to be mined in caves, although be sure to watch out for hot lava.

GAMESWARRIOR VERDICT
An area for more experienced Minecraft players to explore, caves are often the only place to find rare blocks and tough mobs.

MOUNTAINS

Minecraft players looking for a tougher challenge head to mountain biomes. There are seven different versions of these locations, including cherry groves, snowy slopes and jagged peaks. Exploring the mountains will reveal goats, pillager outposts and emerald ore.

GAMESWARRIOR VERDICT
Those who want to survive in mountain biomes will need to be made of really tough stuff and have plenty of resources!

OCEAN & RIVERS

These water-based areas can cover huge amounts of biomes and are often home to unique aquatic mobs, blocks and items. To be able to spend a long time beneath the surface, you'll need to craft a potion of Waterbreathing (see page 48).

GAMESWARRIOR VERDICT
Players who put in plenty of time and effort exploring oceans and rivers will be rewarded with all kinds of underwater goodies!

THE NETHER AND END

The biomes listed on these pages are just some of the locations to explore in the Overworld, preparing players for a real challenge down the line. You can find out everything that you'll need to know about the Nether and the End later on in this game guide!

GAMESWARRIOR VERDICT
Exploring lots of different biomes is a great way to become more experienced, level up and find all kinds of items. The more time you spend in different locations, the better Minecraft player you'll become!

NEW BIOME

GUIDE TO THE PALE GARDEN

The pale garden was revealed by Mojang at Minecraft LIVE 2024 and is an extremely rare and mysterious biome added to the game. It's full of groves of pale oak trees, curtains of hanging moss and a spooky new mob. GamesWarrior is ready to explore this creepy new environment full of surprises!

WHERE TO FIND THE BIOME

The pale garden usually spawns inside dark forests, with the biggest measuring up to 2,000 blocks.

Players can destroy the trees to gain pale oak wood, handy for crafting items.

MOSS AND EYEBLOSSOM

Players can find lots of pale moss in the pale garden, which can spread to other blocks by using bone meal. The biome also includes eyeblossom, a unique flower that closes in the day and opens up at night!

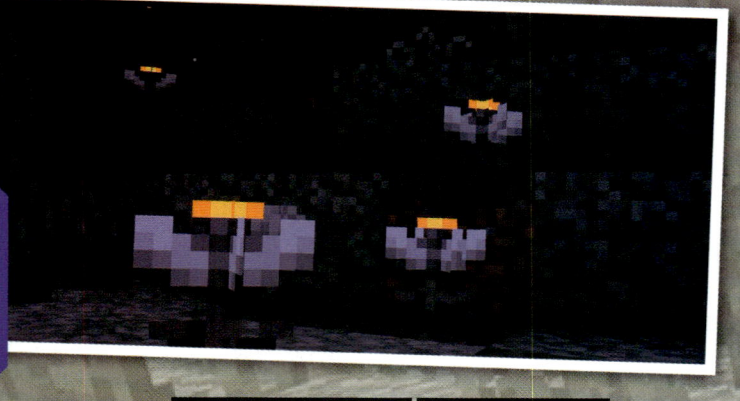

CREAKING HEARTS

Keep your eyes peeled for creaking hearts. These living blocks can be found in pale oak trees and spawn a creaking during night-time and thunderstorms. Breaking the block is the only way to defeat the hostile mob!

GAMESWARRIOR SAYS

The pale garden seems like a creepy biome, but it's a great place for players to grab unique resources such as pale oak wood and eyeblossoms, which are great for decoration. Even the scary mob can be defeated!

MOB PROFILE: CREAKING

FACT-FILE

A creaking will stay completely still before attacking nearby players with headbutts, causing plenty of damage.

The creaking is protected by the creaking heart that spawned it. Smashing that block is the only way to beat the tough foe.

A creaking will stay within a 32-block radius of their creaking heart, so it's sometimes possible to outrun the mob instead of fighting them.

Unfortunately, a creaking doesn't drop any items whatsoever when defeated, making victories much less satisfying.

DAMAGE-ALERT!

A creaking will detect players who walk within 12 blocks of the mob, so be sure to keep your eyes and ears open in order to spot them!

STATS:
- SKILL: ★★★☆☆
- STRENGTH: ★★★★★
- AGILITY: ★★★☆☆
- SPEED: ★★★★☆
- COOLNESS: ★★★★★

OVERALL
★★★★☆

GAMESWARRIOR VERDICT
Scary, but defeatable!

Take a good look at this Minecraft screenshot and see how many creakings you can find!

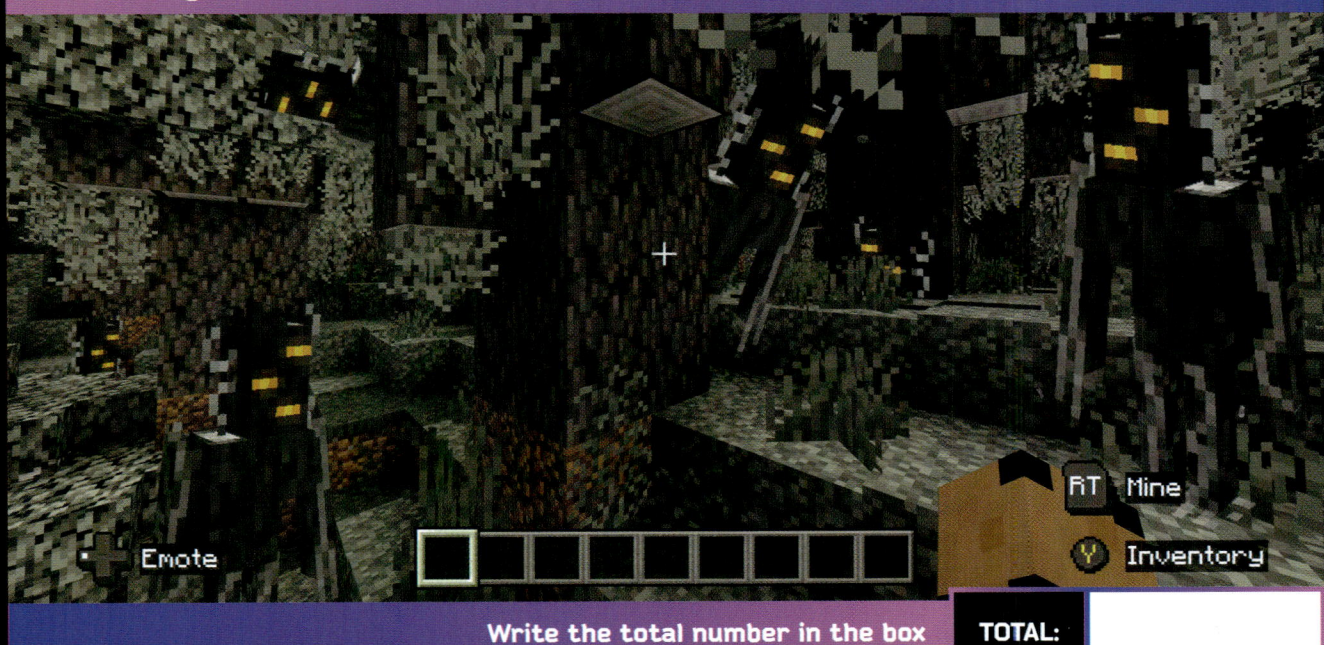

Write the total number in the box TOTAL:

GUIDE TO FRIENDLY MOBS

There are plenty of friendly faces in Minecraft, neutral and passive mobs that won't attack players and can prove to be handy allies. Many of the creatures can be tamed and named. GamesWarrior takes a look at at some of the critters in the Overworld!

BEE

As in the real world, Minecraft bees pollinate flowers and make honey, which can be harvested from beehives... if you're careful!

GAMESWARRIOR VERDICT
Tamed bees make for fun friends once you've attached a lead to them, but make sure to avoid water.

RATING ★★★☆☆

COW

Cows are an essential part of every player's adventure. They supply leather, beef and milk, and you can also find the rare mooshroom variant of the animal in the mushroom fields biome too.

GAMESWARRIOR VERDICT
You'll never run out of nourishing milk again if you have a bucket and a herd of cows!

RATING ★★★★★

CAT

Usually found in villages and swamp huts, this passive mob can be a great pet and they're also very useful for repelling creepers and phantoms.

GAMESWARRIOR VERDICT
With 11 different cat skins in Minecraft, you'll be able to find a feline that's right for you!

RATING ★★★★☆

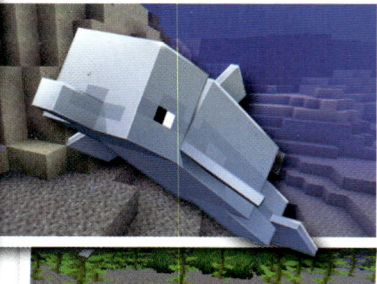

DOLPHIN

When exploring ocean biomes, be sure to swim near a dolphin and you'll get a handy speed boost, which can be useful when avoiding aggressive underwater mobs.

GAMESWARRIOR VERDICT
Try feeding raw cod or raw salmon to a dolphin to make it trust you and lead you to hidden treasure in the sea.

RATING ★★★★★

CHICKEN

Chickens are one of the most essential passive mobs in the game, as they're a great source of raw chicken, feathers and eggs.

GAMESWARRIOR VERDICT

Create your very own chicken farm and you'll be well-stocked with plenty of resources!

RATING ★★★★☆

FROG

There are three different kinds of frogs in Minecraft: temperate, warm and cold. Frogs that eat magma cubes also produce handy froglights.

GAMESWARRIOR VERDICT

Although it's not possible to tame a frog, they will attack some nearby mobs, so can be useful for defence.

RATING ★★★☆☆

GOAT

This neutral mob can usually be found in mountainous biomes, jumping from rock-to-rock. Watch out when approaching them though as they might just ram you!

GAMESWARRIOR VERDICT

Goats are a great source of milk and goat horns, but their screams can get a little annoying at times.

RATING ★★★★☆

IRON GOLEM

Place four iron blocks in a T-shape as shown and add a carved pumpkin or jack o'lantern on top to create an iron golem. This mob will attack any enemies and cause lots of damage.

GAMESWARRIOR VERDICT

An iron golem is the best bodyguard any player can have, but watch out for wild or village versions that may be a threat.

RATING ★★★★★

FOX

Breed two foxes with sweet berries or glow berries and they'll spawn a kit (baby fox) that will trust you, but don't forget to attach a lead so it doesn't run away!

GAMESWARRIOR VERDICT

A tamed fox will defend players from all kinds of hostile threats, including zombies, spiders and wither skeletons.

RATING ★★★★☆

HORSE

Horses are one of the most useful passive mobs in all of Minecraft. Once tamed and saddled, they can be ridden and used to cover large areas of the Overworld at high speed.

GAMESWARRIOR VERDICT

Try to tame a horse as soon as possible, as it's an essential mob to obtain for exploring the wilds of the Overworld.

RATING ★★★★☆

23

LLAMA

Llamas spawn in multiple biomes and appear in four different colours. While it isn't possible to ride this mob, players can still tame them with a lead.

GAMESWARRIOR VERDICT
Llamas are very useful animals, as they can be equipped with a chest and used by players as portable storage!

RATING ★★★★☆

OCELOT

Players can find ocelots in jungle biomes, where the big cat-like mob can be spotted keeping creepers at bay and spawning cute kittens.

GAMESWARRIOR VERDICT
Feed an ocelot raw cod or salmon and it will trust you, which means you can breed more of them.

RATING ★★★☆☆

PANDA

Another unique jungle biome resident is the panda. These bears tend to have different personalities and can be bred to produce panda cubs.

GAMESWARRIOR VERDICT
Pandas love to eat bamboo blocks, so be sure to keep a stash of them nearby at feeding time.

RATING ★★★☆☆

PIG

Not only can players ride a pig once it has a saddle, but they drop porkchops, essential as a food source. Watch out for pigs struck by lightning, as they change into a zombified piglin!

GAMESWARRIOR VERDICT
Be sure to keep a well-stocked pen of pigs and you'll never run short of food or mobs to ride.

RATING ★★★★★

RABBIT

Players may spot various rabbits hopping around the Overworld, including yellow, white, black, brown and combinations of these colors.

GAMESWARRIOR VERDICT
They may be cute, but rabbits are also a handy source of rabbit's foot, rabbit hide and raw rabbit.

RATING ★★★☆☆

SHEEP

As well as dropping raw mutton and wool, sheep can also be bred to produce more of the passive mob and tamed by using a lead.

GAMESWARRIOR VERDICT
See how many different colours of sheep you can add to your collection, including the rare pink version!

RATING ★★★☆☆

TURTLE

Turtles spawn on beaches (in daylight) in groups of five. Turtles drop scutes, which can be used to craft turtle shells and the potion of Turtle Master.

GAMESWARRIOR VERDICT
It's possible to lead a turtle by holding seagrass within 10 blocks of the mob, but they can't be tamed.

RATING ★★★☆☆

WOLF

Wolves can be tamed and will protect their owners from attack. Players are also able to dye the collar around a wolf's neck and even give the creature a name, just like a real pet!

GAMESWARRIOR VERDICT
Wolves will usually teleport to wherever their owner is located, unless in an inaccessible area of the Overworld.

RATING ★★★★★

SNIFFER

One of the more recent mobs to be added to Minecraft, sniffers can be used to find and dig out seeds for all sorts of decorative plants.

GAMESWARRIOR VERDICT
Try breeding two adult sniffers to spawn a snifflet – a baby that's fully grown in around 40 minutes.

RATING ★★★☆☆

VILLAGER

Head to any village in the Overworld to find this passive mob. They'll usually flee from any attackers, but will often drop useful items when dispatched.

GAMESWARRIOR VERDICT
You can cure a zombie villager by giving it the Weakness effect and then a golden apple.

RATING ★★★★☆

BUILDING REVIEW
SEA DIARY

If you want to check out one of the most amazing fan-made Minecraft builds ever, then get ready to dive into the stunning Sea Diary!

UNDER THE SEA

This detailed underwater world has been constructed by Junghan Kim (Owlhouse) and includes a visually-impressive, submerged kingdom that's packed with amazing buildings.

AQUATIC CITY

Sea Diary features a whole aquatic city, complete with structures built into the sides of towering rock formations and embedded into a beautiful coral reef.

SEA LIFE

Junghan's build includes plenty of diverse sea life such as massive creatures, static brick-built animals and plenty of swimming mobs.

AIR SUPPLY

Dotted around Sea Diary are many large, blue spheres, made from smaller blocks. These have been built to look just like big air bubbles!

TIME AND TIDE

Sea Diary took Junghan a total of three years to build, during which time he kept a diary of what it felt like to make such a massive Minecraft world.

SEA STORY

Junghan tried to change the theme and story of Sea Diary a number of times during its creation, switching elements based on the mood and feelings he had at the time.

DEPTH DETAILS

Players who set out to explore the depths of Sea Diary can expect to encounter strange machines, underwater robots, aquatic probes and much more!

MORE WORLDS

If you enjoy Sea Diary, then be sure to check out Junghan's other awesome Minecraft builds including Happy Halloween Jack-o'-lantern City and Tears of Jungle!

CREATE YOUR WORLD

You could try building your own underwater world if you like, starting off small and then adding lots more content as you go.

GAMESWARRIOR VERDICT

Sea Diary looks absolutely incredible and is one of the most amazing Minecraft builds out there!

RATING ★★★★★

CRAFTING RECIPES

Once you've mined and collected enough resources, it's time to start crafting! GamesWarrior have reviewed some special recipes, you'll be able to make everything from armour and weapons to tools and new blocks.

CRAFTING GRID

New players have access to a 2x2 crafting grid into which can be placed various blocks. You'll only be able to make basic resources at the start though, such as turning logs into planks.

GAMESWARRIOR SAYS

Make sure to place items into the correct boxes in the crafting grid in order to make a recipe work.

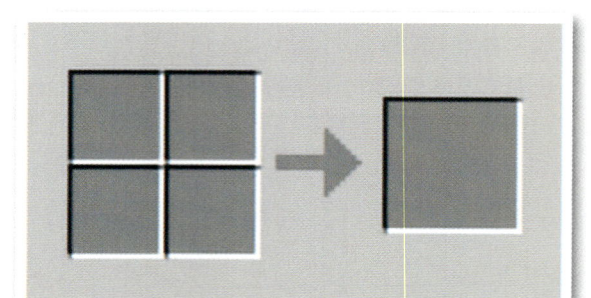

CRAFTING TABLE

Next, you'll need to construct a crafting table using the recipe shown. Once complete, players will have access to a 3x3 crafting grid, allowing them to make more items.

GAMESWARRIOR SAYS

Making a crafting table is the fastest way to level up your Minecraft gaming experience!

RECIPE BOOK

To the left of the crafting table screen is the recipe book. This is a catalogue of recipes unlocked while playing and shows players what they need to craft new items.

GAMESWARRIOR SAYS

You'll know if you've unlocked a new recipe as a notification pops up in the top right-hand corner of the screen.

RECIPE TABS

Recipes are stored in different tabs and show tools, weapons, armour, building materials, food and redstone materials. Clicking on an item shows its recipe in the grid for crafting.

GAMESWARRIOR SAYS
Try clicking on some of the recipe items to discover if they have an alternative pattern design.

START CRAFTING

Add all of the correct items to the crafting grid to proceed with the recipe. Within a few short seconds, you'll have completed crafting and the item can be added to your inventory.

GAMESWARRIOR SAYS
If you craft more than one of each item, a number appears over it to show how many you have.

FIRST ITEMS

As soon as you have your crafting table, use these recipes to make a wooden pickaxe and wooden axe. Having both items will make it much easier to mine for even more essential resources.

GAMESWARRIOR SAYS
The wooden axe is also useful for defending yourself from any hostile mobs you may encounter early on.

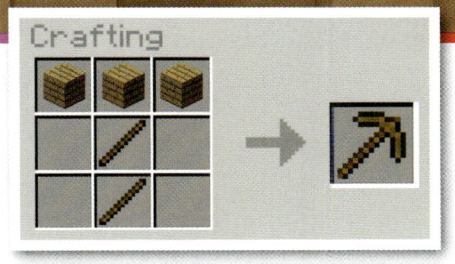

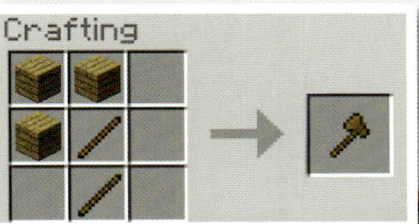

FURNACE

A furnace can be crafted using any eight stone blocks placed in the grid as shown. Once you have a furnace you can start smelting and crafting even better items.

GAMESWARRIOR SAYS
You'll need to add fuel, such as wood or charcoal, to the furnace in order to start smelting recipes.

RECIPES TO TRY!

Deciding what's best to craft in Minecraft can be tricky, but GamesWarrior is here to get you started. Try finding the resources to make the items below and see how fast you can craft them!

SWORD

A basic sword can be crafted using wood planks, stone blocks or iron ingots. Swords can cause damage to mobs and break some blocks, plus they can even be enchanted.

GAMESWARRIOR SAYS

If your sword gets damaged, just place it on the crafting table and it can be easily repaired.

ARMOUR

To defend yourself from attacks, you'll need armour. Protection in the game consists of helmets, chestplates, leggings and boots, all of which can be crafted from different items.

GAMESWARRIOR SAYS

It's even possible to craft armour for your horse or wolf, once you've managed to tame them!

TORCH

When it comes to exploring underground, you'll need a torch to light the way. Craft the item using coal or charcoal and a stick and you'll easily be able to see while mining or at night.

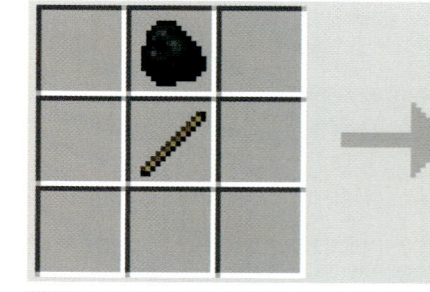

GAMESWARRIOR SAYS

Try making lots of torches and place them on walls – they'll always light your way.

BANNER

If you have six wool blocks from a sheep and a stick, you can craft a banner! Once made, try changing its colour and pattern from the options available in the inventory.

GAMESWARRIOR SAYS
Banners can also be placed in item frames, so you can display them like works of art!

SHIELD

For extra protection, be sure to craft yourself a shield. These tools are very easy to make, but can only be repaired if you've already crafted an anvil and have planks or another shield.

GAMESWARRIOR SAYS
Blocking an attack from a mob using a shield will reduce some damage during combat.

DECORATE YOUR OWN SHIELDS!

Shields can be customised with colourful banners. Grab your pens, pencils or crayons to decorate the templates below.

TRY ADDING BORDERS, STRIPES, SHADING AND PATTERNS IN ANY COLOUR!

GUIDE TO THE DEEP DARK

The deep dark is a recent biome added to Minecraft and offers players a different version of standard caves. The dimly lit location is also the only place to find some unique blocks, but keep your eyes and ears peeled for the lumbering warden!

WHERE TO FIND THE BIOME

Found under mountain areas in the Overworld, the deep dark is below peaks. A small amount of light is generated by sculk catalysts and lava, so you'll need a torch or potion of Night Vision.

SKULK BLOCKS

The deep dark is the only place to find skulk blocks, black cubes with glowing spots. Sneak past skulk sensors carefully or use wool to block the vibrations they detect to avoid activating skulk shriekers which will summon the warden.

ANCIENT CITIES

The deep dark is home to ancient cities, which naturally generate in the biome. These structures contain chests to track down that can include special loot not available anywhere else.

GAMESWARRIOR SAYS

Equipped with sources of light, players can navigate the deep dark but they need to tread carefully.

MOB PROFILE: WARDEN

FACT FILE

Wardens can release a sonic boom that will quickly drain a player's energy and destroy nearby objects.

The good news is that wardens are blind, so you can survive an encounter with them if you sneak past them slowly and quietly!

Try throwing a snowball, arrow or other object away from a warden to create a distraction, before escaping in one piece.

While it is possible to defeat a warden, it will take plenty of time, energy, potions, armour and weapons in order to do so!

DAMAGE ALERT!

Wardens will keep attacking you until you finally beat the mob or manage to run away. Be warned though. Their sonic booms go right through shields and armour!

STATS:
- SKILL: ★★☆☆☆
- STRENGTH: ★★★★★
- AGILITY: ★★★★☆
- SPEED: ★★★★★
- COOLNESS: ★★★★★

OVERALL ★★★★★

GAMESWARRIOR VERDICT
Silent, but deadly!

Use this special code breaker to unscramble the words below and reveal hints that will help you make it safely past the warden!

A. 19 20 5 1 12 20 8 — **STEALTH**
B. 1 22 15 9 4 — **AVOID**
C. 19 14 5 1 11 — **SNEAK**
D. 17 21 9 5 20 12 25 — **QUIETLY**
E. 19 12 15 23 12 25 — **SLOWLY**
F. 19 5 3 18 5 20 12 25 — **SECRETLY**
G. 4 15 4 7 5 — **DODGE**
H. 19 9 4 5 19 20 5 16 — **SIDESTEP**
I. 3 1 18 5 6 21 12 25 — **CAREFULLY**
J. 19 9 12 5 14 20 — **SILENT**

1	2	3	4	5	6	7	8	9	10	11	12	13	14	15	16	17	18	19	20	21	22	23	24	25	26
A	B	C	D	E	F	G	H	I	J	K	L	M	N	O	P	Q	R	S	T	U	V	W	X	Y	Z

THE BEST BLOCKS

There are all kinds of blocks to mine in the Overworld, but some are rarer and more useful than others. Check out the GamesWarrior guide to the best blocks to track down in Minecraft and discover what you can do with them!

STONE
Basic stone blocks are essential for building and can be mined using a pickaxe. In fact, most of the solid blocks in the Overworld are made of stone.

GAMESWARRIOR VERDICT
Fresh stone blocks can actually be made by making lava flow over water.
RATING ★★★★☆

WOOD
This is one of the first blocks players will be able to get in the game by mining trees with their hands or by using an axe for even faster results.

GAMESWARRIOR VERDICT
Wood can be used for crafting all sorts of resources, such as logs, planks and fuel.
RATING ★★★★☆

GLASS
Glass blocks are some of the most useful in the game and can be used when building a shelter, stained different colours and even tinted.

GAMESWARRIOR VERDICT
This is a great block to craft as most mobs can't spawn on or see through them!
RATING ★★★☆☆

PRISMARINE
Only found underwater and in ocean monuments, prismarine blocks change colour from blue to green and make great decorations.

GAMESWARRIOR VERDICT
Add prismarine to your block collection and you'll soon discover it's a high blast-resistant item.
RATING ★★★☆☆

SEA LANTERN
You'll need a tool enchanted with Silk Touch to mine sea lanterns, but it's worth it as the glowing blocks can be a handy light source.

GAMESWARRIOR VERDICT
Sea lanterns emit the brightest light of any block in Minecraft, so be sure to grab some if you can!
RATING ★★★★☆

CORAL
Another block that needs to be mined with a Silk Touch enchanted tool is coral, a decorative item that comes in five different colours.

GAMESWARRIOR VERDICT
Try adding coral to your underwater builds and your friends will be really surprised with how they look.
RATING ★★★★☆

PURPUR
Keep an eye out in the End for these purple cubes. Purpur blocks are what end cities and end ships are made from and are decorative items.

GAMESWARRIOR VERDICT
Try impressing your mates with a base that's completely made out of purpur blocks!
RATING ★★★☆☆

BLUE ICE
While normal ice blocks can be melted, blue ice is solid and can stay that way. Head to the bottom of an iceberg or snowy tundra village to find them.

GAMESWARRIOR VERDICT
Nearly all mobs will slip and slide on blue ice, so the blocks can come in handy as a defensive barrier.
RATING ★★★★☆

DIAMOND ORE
These rare blocks generate deep underground. You'll need an iron pickaxe or better to mine them, but when the block breaks it drops multiple diamonds!

GAMESWARRIOR VERDICT
One of the strongest blocks in Minecraft, use it to craft armour, weapons and much more!
RATING ★★★★★

ANCIENT DEBRIS

This rare ore is located in the Nether, where it can be mined using a diamond pickaxe and used to craft fireproof items.

GAMESWARRIOR VERDICT

Be sure to smelt ancient debris in a furnace in order to gain netherite scraps

RATING ★★★★☆

EMERALD ORE

Possibly the rarest block in Minecraft, emerald ore only generates in mountains and windswept hill biomes and needs to be mined with an iron pickaxe.

GAMESWARRIOR VERDICT

Use emerald ore to craft truly stunning armour and weapons!

RATING ★★★★★

END PORTAL FRAME

Players can only find end portal frames in underground strongholds in the Overworld. Place 12 blocks in a rectangle to access the End dimension.

GAMESWARRIOR VERDICT

Don't forget you'll also need 12 eyes of ender to place in the frame in order to activate the portal.

RATING ★★★★☆

NETHER BRICK

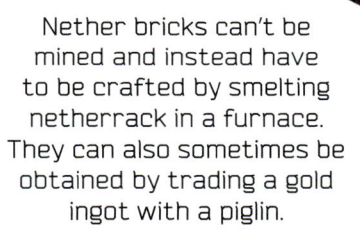

Nether bricks can't be mined and instead have to be crafted by smelting netherrack in a furnace. They can also sometimes be obtained by trading a gold ingot with a piglin.

GAMESWARRIOR VERDICT

This tough, non-flammable block is ideal for creating strong bases!

RATING ★★★★☆

OBSIDIAN

When water flows over lava in the game, it can create obsidian. The blocks are resistant to explosions and can be used to craft a nether portal frame.

GAMESWARRIOR VERDICT

You'll need a diamond pickaxe to mine obsidian, but the tough blocks are worth obtaining.

RATING ★★★★☆

DRAGON HEAD

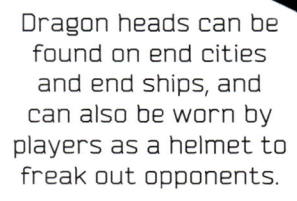

Dragon heads can be found on end cities and end ships, and can also be worn by players as a helmet to freak out opponents.

GAMESWARRIOR VERDICT

Add a redstone block to a dragon head and the block's mouth will open and close!

RATING ★★★★☆

LODESTONE

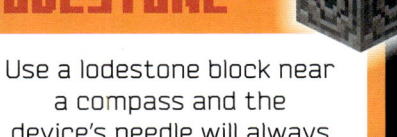

Use a lodestone block near a compass and the device's needle will always point to the block, making it a useful item to find your way back home.

GAMESWARRIOR VERDICT

A lodestone compass can be a handy tool for finding your way out of jungle biomes!

RATING ★★★★☆

CONDUIT

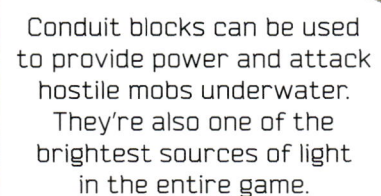

Conduit blocks can be used to provide power and attack hostile mobs underwater. They're also one of the brightest sources of light in the entire game.

GAMESWARRIOR VERDICT

Conduits restore nearby players' oxygen, give underwater night vision and increase mining speed.

RATING ★★★★☆

END STONE

Located in the End, these naturally occurring blocks make up all of the ground in the realm. They're also blast-resistant which makes them very handy indeed.

GAMESWARRIOR VERDICT

End stones cannot be destroyed by the ender dragon, so are useful for defence against the mob.

RATING ★★★★☆

BUILDING STEP-BY-STEP
ULTIMATE OVERWORLD BASE

If you're looking to get started with an epic Minecraft build, then GamesWarrior has you covered. Just follow our step-by-step guide across these pages and you too can make your very own ultimate Overworld base in Survival or Creative modes!

1 To kick things off, try to find yourself a clear, safe and open space somewhere in the Overworld. It should be as flat as possible, with no obstructions that may slow down the building process.

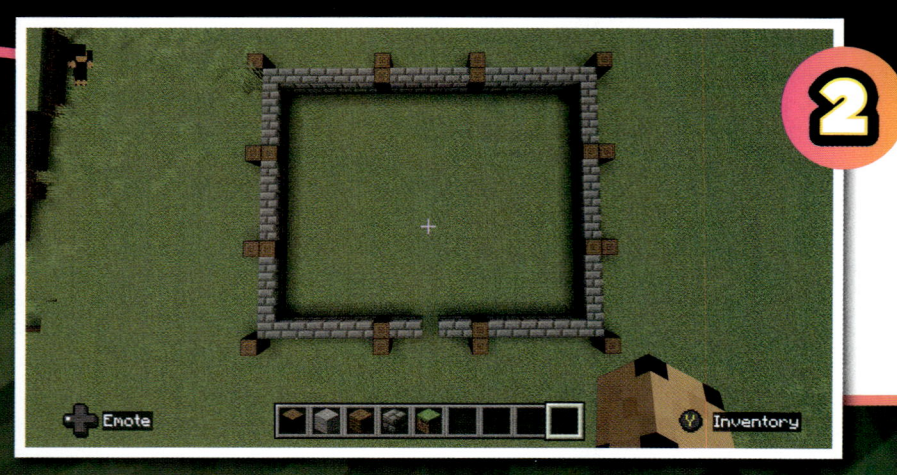

2 Next, start off by using lots of sturdy blocks to create the rectangular foundations of your base. We've gone for tough bricks and spruce logs, but you can use whatever you may have.

3 Now, head inside the foundations of your base and start digging out the floor. We recommend going one block down and placing wood blocks, such as the spruce planks shown in this image.

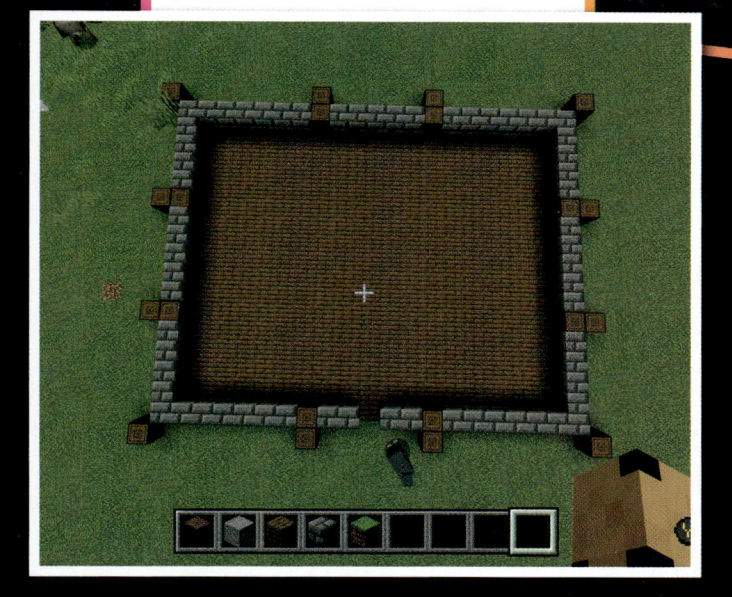

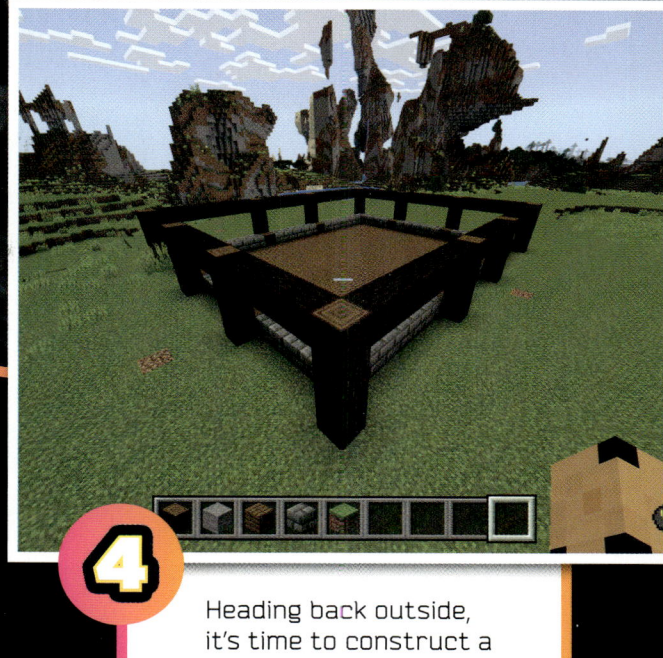

4 Heading back outside, it's time to construct a wooden frame around your base. You could try making it with spruce logs, like we have, or any other wood blocks will do.

5 Begin building up the exterior walls, one layer at a time. Don't forget to leave room for windows and especially a door, otherwise you won't be able to get back inside!

6 Now, start adding in all of the windows by using glass panes. We've also placed a decorative spruce door at the front of the base, but you can use any materials you like.

7 The first floor of your building will need some attention next. We've gone with more tough bricks again here, with spruce fences around the outside of the area to make this section really stand out.

8 For the next stage of your base, add in spruce log pillars on the roof, or any other wooden blocks that you may have. These will help you mark out the area for the first floor you'll be making on top.

9 Add plenty of tough bricks for the walls on the first floor and the rest of the spruce logs. Your base will definitely also need a roof adding to stop the rain getting in!

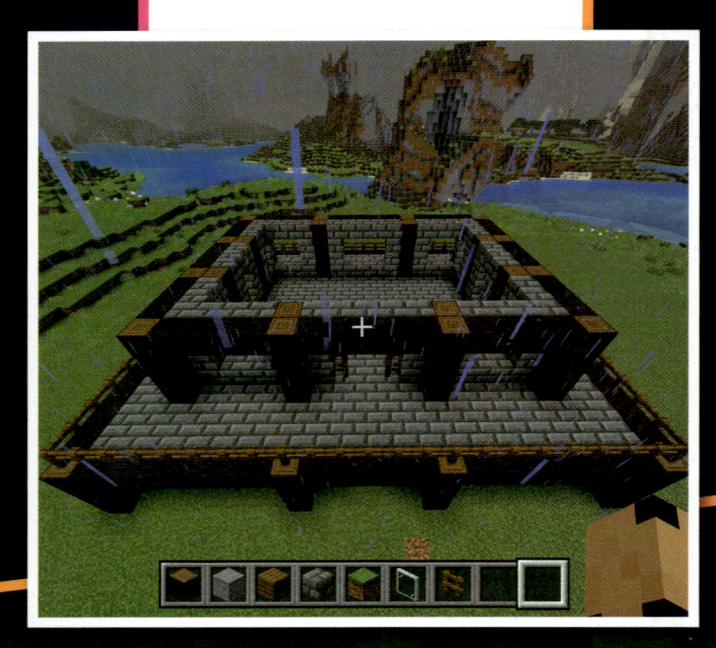

10 Place lots of tough brick stairs or other stair blocks all over this section of your base. They'll help to give the finished roof an impressive, slanted appearance.

38

11 Complete the roof area of your base by adding in lots of spruce stairs or other stair blocks. You'll end up with a look that contrasts the wood with the stone for a really distinctive look.

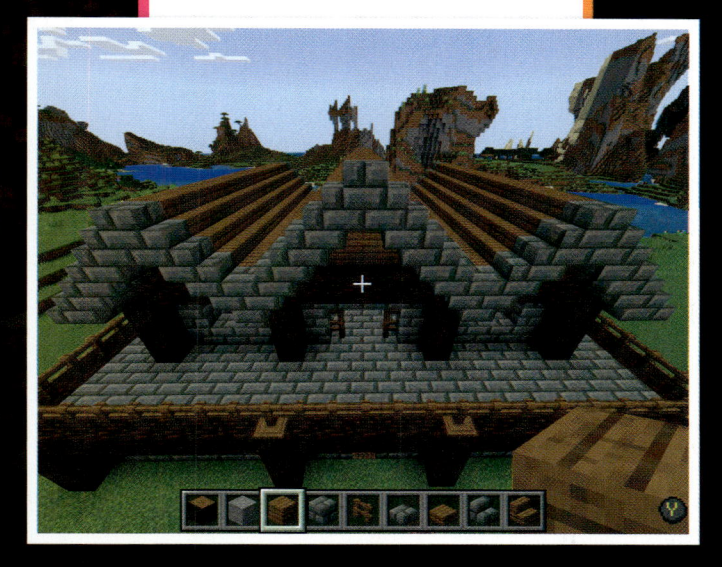

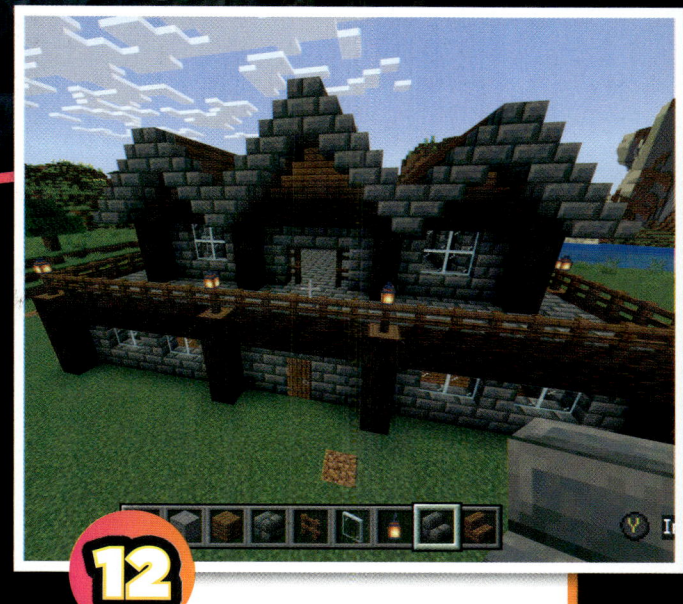

12 The first floor area of your base can be further improved with glass panes placed in the windows and lanterns dotted around the spruce fences, providing light at night-time.

13 Now head down to the ground floor again and begin constructing a sturdy stone wall around the base. We've used chiselled tough bricks here, so that the wall looks a little different to the main build.

14 You'll also want to add in some tough bricks all around the edge of your base, otherwise the wooden sections of the building will catch fire later on!

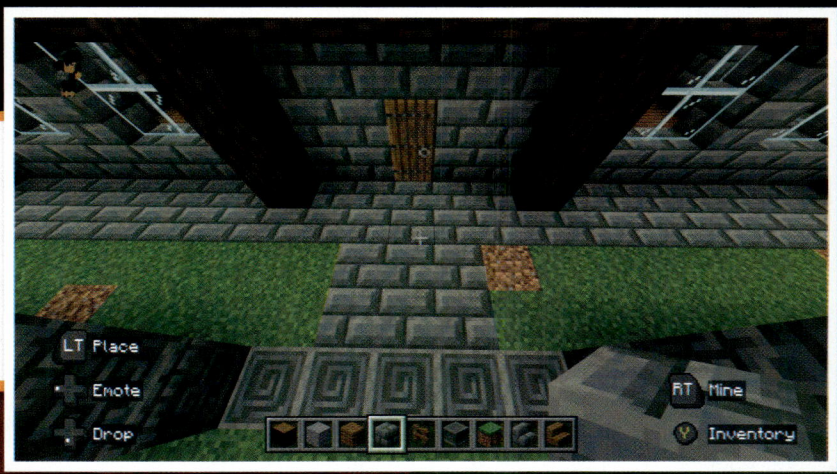

15

Dig one block down around the inside of your base's wall, removing all the grass blocks. Once you've cleared all of that space, fill it in with plenty of red-hot lava.

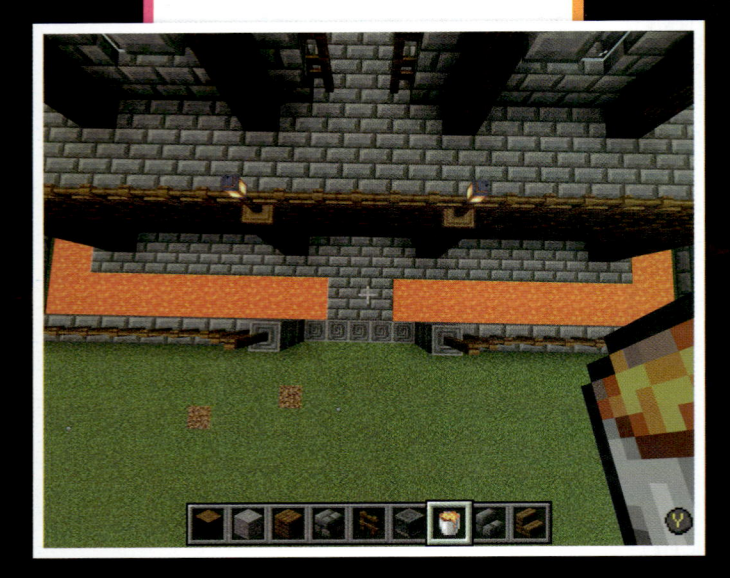

16

It's time to step inside the house now and add some interior features. We've placed two sets of tough brick stairs side-by-side, with openings in the floor above for easy access.

17

For a fun feature, clear out one brick in the ceiling of the first floor and then another directly below on the ground floor. Now, place a bucket of water above to create your very own waterfall!

18

Next, feel free to add as many decorations and items inside your house as you like. For this section we've gone with some book shelves, a handy crafting table, a kitchen area and more.

19 For the other side of the ground floor, we've created a fun treasure area. Included in this section are precious gold, diamond, emerald blocks and chests, as well as two sets of gold armour!

19 For the finishing touches to our ultimate Overworld base, we've placed two flags outside the main entrance, which have been created by using red wool blocks.

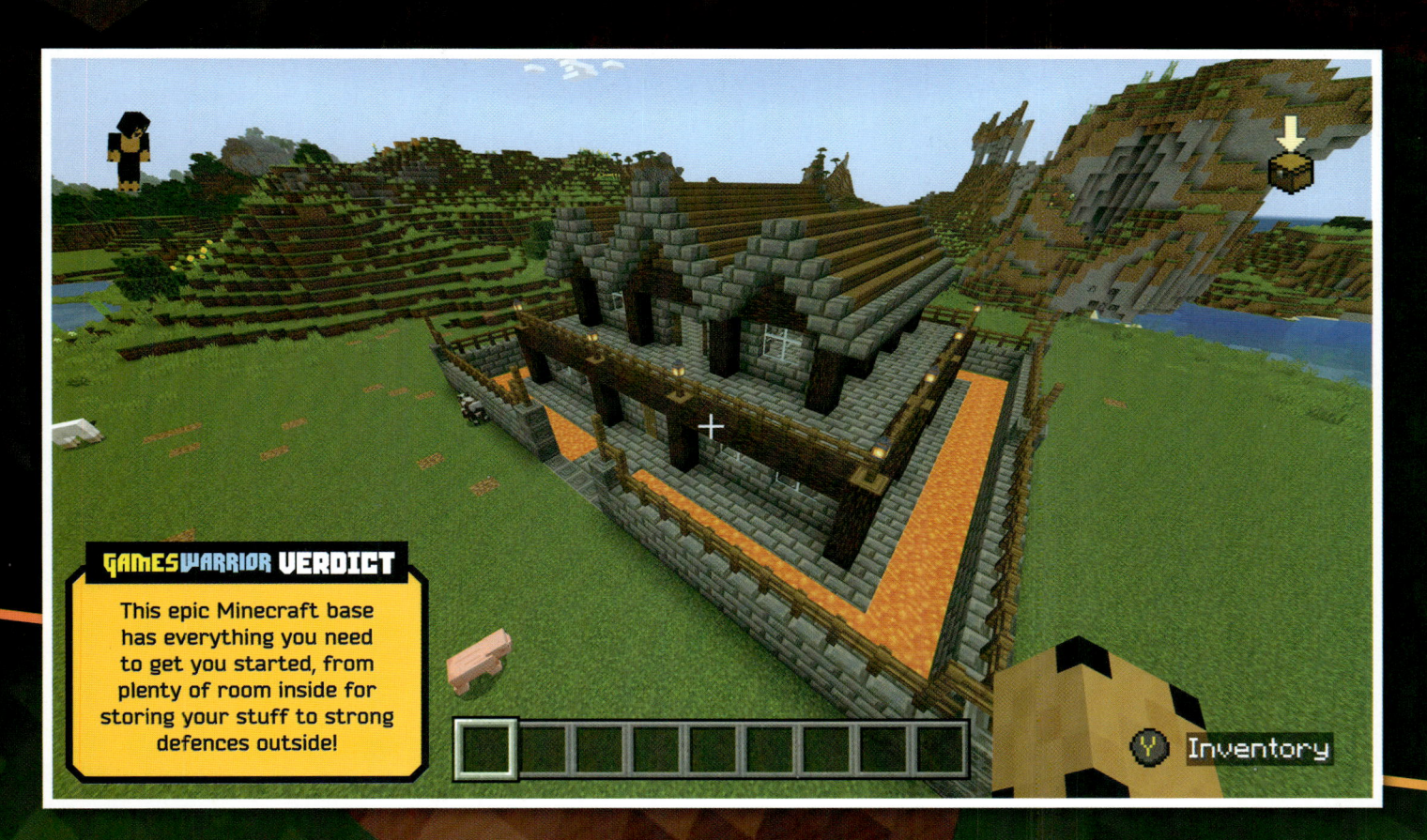

GAMESWARRIOR VERDICT

This epic Minecraft base has everything you need to get you started, from plenty of room inside for storing your stuff to strong defences outside!

GUIDE TO THE TRIAL CHAMBERS

If you're looking for a real Minecraft challenge, get ready to tackle trial chambers. These structures can be found deep underground and you'll need a trial explorer map to find them. Read on to discover GamesWarrior's guide to surviving the the various tests to pick up exclusive loot and armour trims!

TRACK THE TRIALS

Try to find a cartographer in a village or craft yourself a cartography table to turn a villager into one. Cartographers will then give you a trial explorer map to find the hidden chambers.

GAMESWARRIOR SAYS
You may need to dig deep to find a trial chamber, but they're well-worth the effort!

THE BOGGED AND BREEZE

Players will get to fight tough skeleton variants called the bogged and a new hostile mob, the breeze, which use strong blasts of wind to blow you away.

GAMESWARRIOR VERDICT
Bring your best weapons, armour and food to a trial chamber, as you'll need them to beat these mobs!

DANGER RATING ★★★★☆

TRIAL SPAWNERS

There are lots of trial spawners throughout the chambers and each one spawns a number of mobs depending on how many players are nearby.

GAMESWARRIOR SAYS

Even more mobs will appear as you defeat them, but they have a limit and will run out.

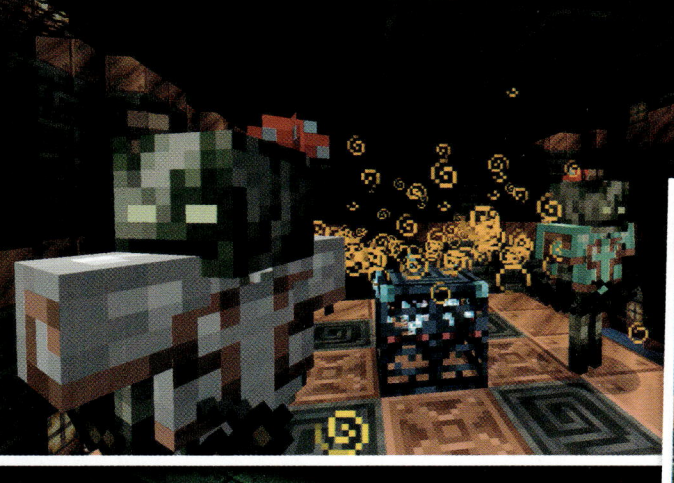

LOTS OF LOOT

Beat each challenge to receive special loot or trial key to unlock vault blocks which contain even more exclusive items!

GAMESWARRIOR SAYS

Sometimes you'll pick up an ominous key which can be used to open an ominous vault.

43

GUIDE TO TRIAL CHAMBER MOBS

Trial spawners will continually add lots more mobs to trial chambers, including these challenging enemies to defeat! GamesWarrior has identified some tricky mobs to look out for!

BREEZE

This floating hostile mob can be quite tough to beat at first, as it attacks from a distance using powerful blasts of wind that cause lots of damage.

GAMESWARRIOR VERDICT

Defeating a breeze is well-worth it, as the mob drops breeze rods which can be crafted into wind charges and maces!

DANGER RATING ★★★★☆

BOGGED

A skeleton variant, bogged regularly pop up in swamp biomes. This undead mob shoots arrows of poison, so be sure you have plenty of potions of Healing!

GAMESWARRIOR VERDICT

Bogged may look tough to beat, but they're actually much slower to reload their bows than normal skeletons.

DANGER RATING ★★★☆☆

HUSK

This zombie variant usually spawns in desert biomes, but can also sometimes appear in trial chambers. They don't burn in sunlight though and inflict a Hunger status effect on players.

GAMESWARRIOR VERDICT

If you can avoid getting overwhelmed by too many husks, defeated foes drop iron ingots, carrots, potatoes and rotten flesh.

RATING ★★★☆☆

BLAZE

Usually found in nether fortresses, blazes fire a trio of fireballs or attack players with their spinning rods if they get too close.

GAMESWARRIOR VERDICT

Although tricky to beat, this mob is the only source of blaze rods, essential for crafting eyes of ender.

DANGER RATING ★★★★☆

Find your way out of the tricky trial chamber maze to reach the treasure chest at the end, but watch out for hostile mobs!

START

45

GAMESWARRIOR REVIEW
MINECRAFT MOVIE

One of the biggest films of 2025, *A Minecraft Movie* proved to be a smash hit at the box office. Fans across the globe joined Jack Black as Steve in an epic big screen adventure that was packed with mobs, laughs and even a few songs!

JOURNEY TO THE OVERWORLD

In *A Minecraft Movie*, a group of misfits travel from the human world to a blocky realm to face off against a horde of piglins that want to conquer the Overworld.

STEVE!

Along the way they encounter Steve, a bearded human who has spent years in the Overworld, learning to master crafting and discovering both the Orb of Dominance and the Earth Crystal.

GARRETT GARRISON

Jason Momoa's hilarious character is Garrett 'The Garbage Man' Garrison, a former video game champion who still thinks he has what it takes to be a winner!

DENNIS

A Minecraft Movie also features Dennis, Steve's pet wolf. Tamed with a collar, this mob is so loyal that Steve even sings a special song about Dennis at one point!

TM & © 2025 Warner Bros. Entertainment Inc. All rights reserved.

PROMO CODES

Fans who booked tickets to watch *A Minecraft Movie* could grab a code for an in-game jetpack. Fast food retailer McDonald's also offered up codes for exclusive skins too!

MOVIE DLC

Mojang joined in with all of the *A Minecraft Movie* fun by offering up a selection of exciting DLC. Content included skin packs, items such as the potato launcher and even lava chicken.

YOUTUBE CELEBS

Did you know that *A Minecraft Movie* includes cameos from YouTube celebrities including DanTDM, Aphmau, Mumbo Jumbo and LDShadowLady?

CHICKEN JOCKEY!

Some cinema-goers were very excited when one particular mob appeared on screen. The chicken jockey scene proved to be a fan-favourite moment that went viral worldwide!

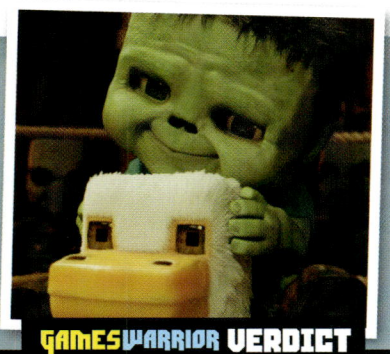

GAMESWARRIOR VERDICT

An epic, laugh-out loud film bringing the Overworld to life for millions of fans to enjoy!

What was your favourite moment?

RARE SPAWN!

What two Minecraft characters would you merge together? Use this space to draw a picture of your ultimate mob combo!

GUIDE TO ENCHANTMENTS & POTIONS

GamesWarrior have reviewed what players need to master the art of enchanting and how to brew potions, to take their gaming to the next level!

ENCHANTING

Enchanting is a mechanic that allows players to augment their own armour, tools, weapons and books, making them much stronger.

GAMESWARRIOR VERDICT
It's easy to spot any items that have been enchanted, as they receive special glint animation that makes them shine.

ENCHANTING TABLE

There are four different ways to obtain an enchanted item in Survival mode, but the easiest is to craft an enchanting table using the recipe on this page.

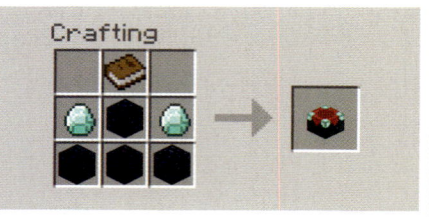

GAMESWARRIOR VERDICT
Using an enchanting table is a great method to use, but you will need to exchange experience points and lapis lazuli to do so.

HOW TO ENCHANT

To begin enchanting an item, place it into one of the enchanting table's inventory slots and add lapis lazuli in the other, then choose which enchantment option you want to use.

GAMESWARRIOR VERDICT
Enchanting is a great, but you'll need to be experience level 1 to do so and items can only be boosted up to level 30.

48

ANVIL ENCHANTING

Another way to enchant is to craft an anvil (with the recipe below), then combine an enchanted book with an item or two of the same item with existing enchantments.

GAMESWARRIOR VERDICT
Enchanting two existing items into one is a great idea, as the new item then has the enchantments of both!

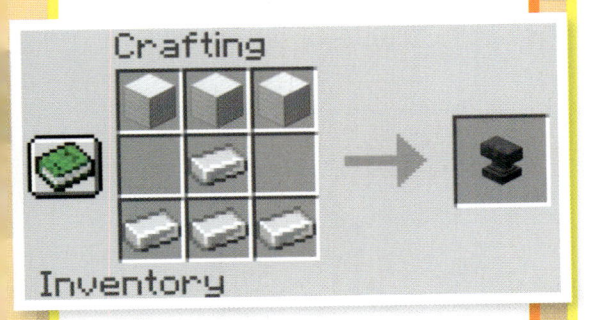

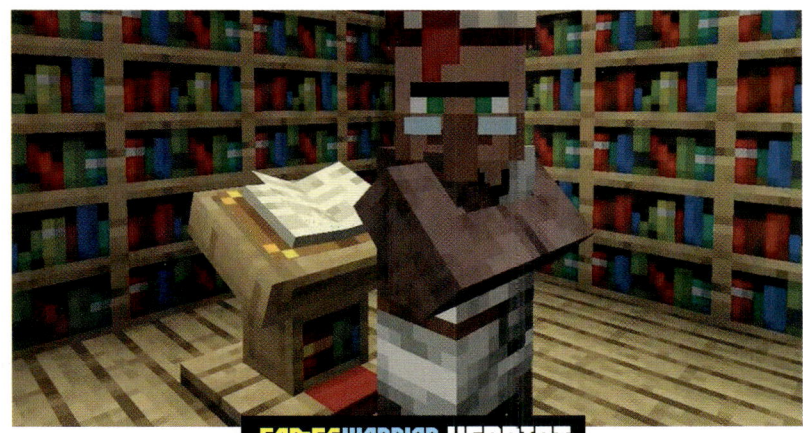

LIBRARIAN VILLAGER

The final enchantment method available in Minecraft is to take any books you have to a librarian villager, who may enchant them in exchange for precious emeralds.

GAMESWARRIOR VERDICT
Librarian villagers can come in very handy for enchanting items quickly and easily!

DISENCHANTING

The only way to disenchant an item is by using the grindstone or by repairing them by using the crafting grid. This can sometimes be handy if you've picked up a cursed item.

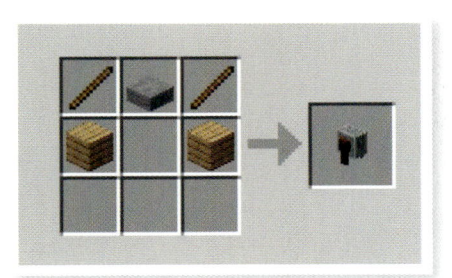

GAMESWARRIOR VERDICT
Having a grindstone in your inventory can definitely be useful if any of your items are ever cursed.

ENCHANTED ITEMS

It's also possible to find enchanted items in the wild, such as by trading with a villager, fishing, opening treasure chests or by defeating mobs such as zombies, piglins and strays.

GAMESWARRIOR VERDICT
There's nothing more satisfying than stumbling across enchanted items in End cities, shipwrecks, temples and other locations!

BREWING POTIONS

Another handy ability in Minecraft is brewing, allowing you to create various magical potions using a crafted brewing stand as shown.

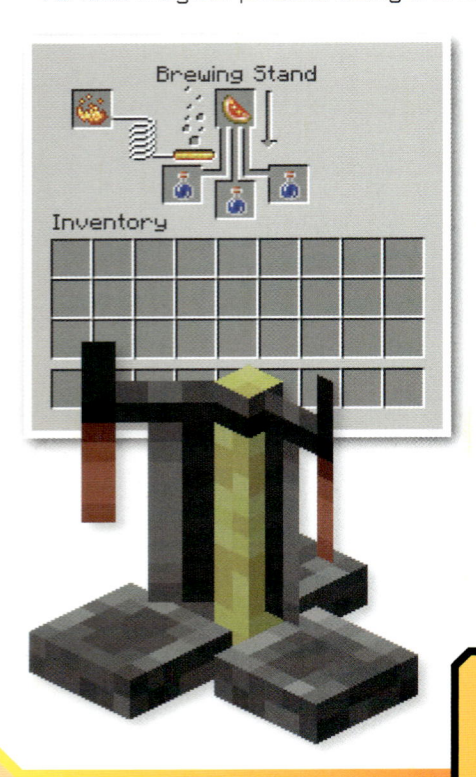

GAMESWARRIOR VERDICT
Brewing stands are essential for making potions, but be sure to craft plenty of water bottles in advance to store them all!

BREWING EQUIPMENT

In addition to the brewing stand, you're going to need to craft a cauldron and make sure your inventory is stocked with plenty of water and blaze powder.

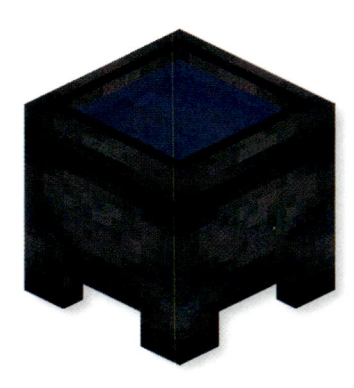

GAMESWARRIOR VERDICT
A cauldron can hold more water than a brewing stand, although placing them near a source of water first is always a good idea.

BASE INGREDIENTS

You'll need certain base ingredients to brew any potion, including nether wart, redstone dust, glowstone dust, fermented spider eyes, gunpowder and dragon's breath.

GAMESWARRIOR VERDICT
With the items above you'll be able to make base potions and then adding an extra ingredient to create various effects and cures.

POTION TYPES

There are all kinds of different potions in the game, some that can give you special abilities such as Invisibility and Water Breathing, and others that affect mobs.

GAMESWARRIOR VERDICT
Try adding all kinds of different ingredients to your own potions to find out what kind of unique effects they may have!

SPLASH POTIONS

Splash potions can be thrown, making them handy for players to use on nearby mobs. They explode on impact and affect entities for a limited time.

GAMESWARRIOR VERDICT
Having a decent stock of Splash potions can be very useful if you're ever overwhelmed by large groups of mobs or don't have any weapons.

LINGERING POTIONS

Using a Lingering potion creates a cloud of particles that lasts for up to 30 seconds. Any mobs that pass through the cloud during that time will be affected.

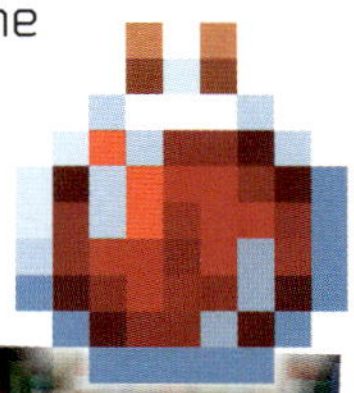

GAMESWARRIOR VERDICT
Lingering potions are doubly useful, as players can also stand in the cloud area to gain the benefits of an effect!

ENCHANTMENT EXPERT

Match the enchantment on the left to the correct item on the right!

- FEATHER FALLING
- FIRE ASPECT
- LUCK OF THE SEA
- SILK TOUCH
- IMPALING

- SWORD
- TRIDENT
- ARMOUR
- SHOVEL
- FISHING ROD

GUIDE TO THE NETHER

More experienced players can take their Minecraft gaming to the next level by visiting the Nether. Filled with fire, lava and dangerous mobs, read on to discover GamesWarrior's thoughts on this strange dimension and the plenty of useful items to be found there too!

WHERE TO FIND THE BIOME

To access the Nether, you'll need to construct a nether portal in the Overworld. These are made from a rectangular frame of obsidian, then activated using fire or flint and steel.

GAMESWARRIOR SAYS
These handy constructs are the only way in and out of the Nether, so don't destroy them!

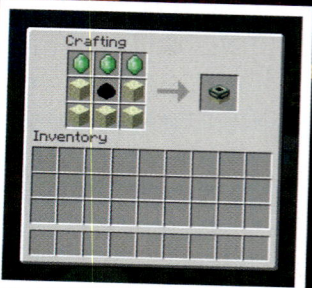

BIOMES

The Nether is divided into a few different biomes. These include the nether wastes, crimson forest, warped forest, soul sand valley and basalt deltas, all of which are worth exploring to find items.

GAMESWARRIOR SAYS
There's plenty to check out in each of the Nether biomes, so be sure to spend plenty of time looking around.

MAJOR DANGER

If you're not prepared to tackle the Nether in advance, you could be in trouble. This dimension is full of dangers, so take plenty of supplies, water, weapons and armour.

GAMESWARRIOR SAYS
Golden apples are a great source of healing and you'll need them to battle the wither!

NETHER STRUCTURES

Nether biomes feature unique structures such as the nether fortress, bastion remnant and ruined portal. A nether fortress is the only place where blazes and wither skeletons spawn!

GAMESWARRIOR SAYS

Check out bastion remnants and you'll usually find a large amount of gold blocks and loot chests inside.

TRANSPORT

Striders can be tamed and ridden by using a fishing rod, a saddle and some nearby warped fungus, then head down to a lava lake to secure your ride.

GAMESWARRIOR SAYS

Take a couple of boats with you into the Nether, as they can help you slide off cliffs without taking fall damage!

NETHER MOBS

The nether dimension can spawn all kinds of hostile mobs such as enderman, ghasts, hoglins, magma cubes, piglins, striders, skeletons, wither skeletons and zombified piglins.

GAMESWARRIOR SAYS

If you have any enchantments, try using them to boost your armour and weapons before you visit the Nether.

UNIQUE BLOCKS

Some blocks can only be mined in the Nether. These include netherrack, nether quartz ore, warped stem and fungus, magma blocks, glowstone, blackstone, soul soil and lots more.

GAMESWARRIOR SAYS

Many normal blocks from the Overworld won't act the same in the Nether, so look around for local resources.

NAVIGATION

Compasses and clocks spin crazily and maps don't work at all in the Nether. Try placing block markers on your journey, to remind you where you've come from.

GAMESWARRIOR SAYS

Place a jack o'lantern block in the Nether and it will always point to the direction of your base!

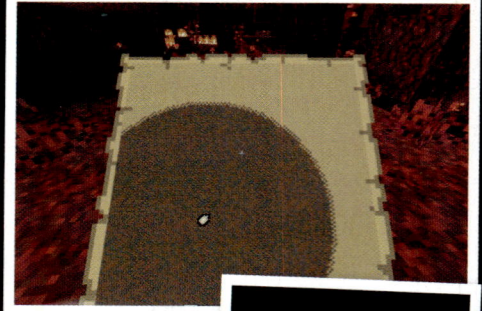

NETHER BASES

One of the first things you should try to do when entering the Nether is build a base or clear out a nether fortress. Try making your own structure to defend from constant mob attacks.

GAMESWARRIOR SAYS

You could always try adding defences to your base, which can help keep those hostile mobs at bay!

BLAZE SPAWNERS

Nether fortresses contain blaze spawners that generate the hostile mob. However, simply place torches on the block and they will prevent any more blazes from spawning.

GAMESWARRIOR SAYS

You can always destroy a blaze spawner with a pickaxe, but if you do you won't be able to farm blazes in the fortress.

BARTERING

If you have any gold ingots, it's possible to barter with piglins, which stops them getting angry with you. The mob can reward you with Fire Resistance potions, obsidian and more.

GAMESWARRIOR SAYS

Make sure not to drop any gold ingots on the ground, as piglins will pick them up but not give you anything in return!

MOB PROFILE: WITHER

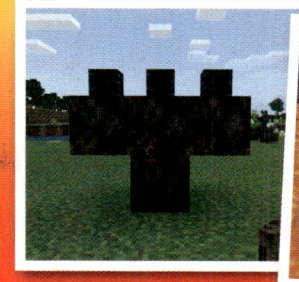

Easily one of the most destructive mobs in Minecraft, the wither is tough to beat even if you are a gaming pro!

FACT-FILE

A wither can only be spawned by Minecraft players and requires four blocks of soul sand or soul soil in a 'T' shape.

You'll also need three wither skeleton skulls, which can only be found by locating and defeating the mob in a nether fortress!

The last block to be placed on top has to be the wither skeleton skull, which then triggers the mob with a massive explosion.

YOU·WILL·NEED...

...an enchanted weapon and armour to take on the wither, plus plenty of healing potions and golden apples.

If you manage to defeat a wither, it will drop a nether star. This rare item can be used for crafting beacons.

STATS:

- SKILL: ★★★★☆
- STRENGTH: ★★★★★
- AGILITY: ★★★★☆
- SPEED: ★★★★★
- COOLNESS: ★★★★★

OVERALL
★★★★★

GAMESWARRIOR VERDICT
Spawn this lethal mob... if you dare!

DAMAGE·ALERT!

There's no easy way to beat a wither, but it's worth it if you do. Keep moving, attack from a distance and heal whenever you can!

VILLAGERS AND TRADING

If there are certain items that players are looking for in Minecraft but can't find them, then they can always try trading with Villagers and Wandering Traders. GamesWarrior has reviewed what they might need for their Overworld transactions!

EMERALDS

Before you can start any trades with villagers, you'll need to mine some emeralds. These are rarer than diamonds, but can sometimes be found in chests if you look hard enough.

FIRST TRADE

To begin a trade, simply head to a nearby village, walk up to a villager and select 'Use'. A menu will then open up that shows you exactly what kind of items the villager has for sale.

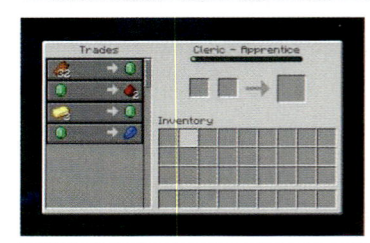

VILLAGER ITEMS

Villagers offer a wide range of items for you to buy and are the only way to obtain globe banner patterns, and woodland and ocean explorer maps in Survival mode.

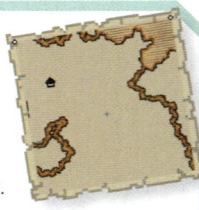

GAMESWARRIOR VERDICT
It can sometimes be tricky finding enough emeralds to trade with, so digging deep and searching far and wide is the best way to find them.

GAMESWARRIOR VERDICT
While most trades can be straightforward, it can be a bit annoying if a villager is attacked during a transaction as the sale then ends.

GAMESWARRIOR VERDICT
Villagers are a great source of renewable items such as bells, diamond gear, lapis lazuli, bottles o' enchanting, glass, sand, coral blocks and more!

WANDERING TRADERS

If you're not near a village, you may still encounter a wandering trader.

This passive mob randomly spawns in the Overworld, so keep your eyes peeled for them.

It's worth noting that wandering traders will always despawn after 40 minutes (two full Minecraft days), so make sure you've picked up the items you want from them first.

GAMESWARRIOR VERDICT
Wandering traders usually appear with two leashed llamas in tow, which means they can carry plenty of items for you to trade with.

GAMESWARRIOR VERDICT
Wandering traders have six random trades, so you never know exactly what items they may have until you start your sale with them.

CAREER LEVELS

All villagers have a total of five career levels, which increase the more you trade with them. Trades reward both the player and villager with essential experience points.

VILLAGER PROFESSIONS

A villager's profession affects what kind of items the mob can trade. For instance, villagers wearing straw hats are farmers, giving them access to wheat, vegetables, fruit and other produce.

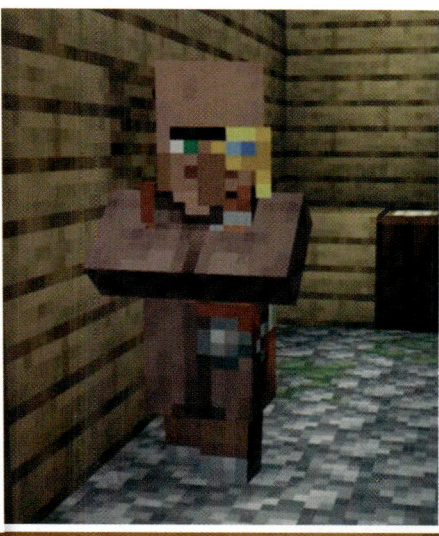

GAMESWARRIOR VERDICT
Each time a villager's career levels up, two new trades become available, although their items will still eventually run out of stock at some point.

GAMESWARRIOR VERDICT
You never know what profession a villager will have until you interact with them, so trading with as many of the mob as possible is a good idea!

NON-TRADING VILLAGERS

Did you know that not all villagers can trade? It's true! Nitwits and unemployed villagers will just shake their heads and grunt if they don't have a job.

GAMESWARRIOR VERDICT
While there's always a chance that you'll bump into a nitwit or an unemployed villager, most villagers will usually have a useful profession.

DISCOUNTS

Players can get discounts from certain villagers if they have a good reputation with them. For instance, curing zombie villagers will definitely get you in their good books!

GAMESWARRIOR VERDICT
Try to avoid killing villagers as you never know when you might need to trade with them for essential items and supplies.

ITEM PRICES

The prices of all kinds of items can rise and fall while you're playing Minecraft. The good news is that price changes will only affect the first item in any trade.

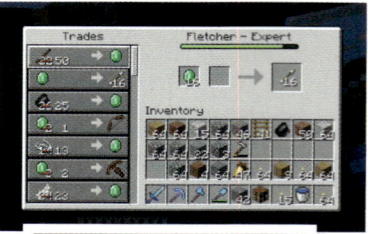

GAMESWARRIOR VERDICT
Watch for sold out items increasing in price the next time they're back in stock, and be sure to carry plenty of emeralds!

HERO OF THE VILLAGE

Players who manage to defeat a raid gain the Hero of the Village status. This reward includes gifts from villagers and useful discounts on trades for up to 40 minutes.

Challenge Complete!
Hero of the Village

GAMESWARRIOR VERDICT
It's a good idea to make as many trades as you can while the Hero of the Village status effect has been activated.

TRADING TANGLE

Follow the tangled lines below to work out which items the villager is trading!

BELL

GOLDEN APPLE

EXPLORER MAP

LAPIS LAZULI ORE

CORAL BLOCK

59

TREASURES OF THE OVERWORLD

The Overworld is where players start their Minecraft adventure and the place where they learn to become a pro player. GamesWarrior has identified everything that this location has to offer and how players will be spending their time there!

OVERWORLD OVERVIEW

The main realm players first encounter is the Overworld, an above-ground biome that can feature all kinds of terrain, vegetation, weather and mobs.

SEEDS

Each time a player starts a new game, the levels will burst forth from a randomly-generated seed. That starting point decides what the Overworld biome will ultimately look like.

BIOMES

There are over 60 different types of Overworld biomes and you can read more about each on pages 16 to 19. They contain structures such as mountains, lakes and even floating islands!

DAYLIGHT CYCLE

During the day, the sun lights up biomes and makes it easier to get around, while night-time is much darker and more dangerous.

MOBS

While wandering around the Overworld, players will encounter different mobs. These can be friendly, neutral mobs or hostile foes in the shape of zombies, witches and creepers!

BLOCKS

There are all kinds of useful blocks to be found in the Overworld. From dirt, wood and stone to powder snow, copper ore and bamboo, there are plenty of resources to collect and use.

BUILD A BASE

One of the first things that players should build in the Overworld is a base. This should be one that gives you shelter from the weather, a place to sleep and plenty of protection from attacking mobs.

TRANSPORTATION

Getting around the Overworld can sometimes be time-consuming, but there is transportation. Try taming a pig, horse or camel to ride, or craft a boat to explore water.

BUILD A BETTER BASE

Try adding furniture, more rooms, extra levels and a moat to your base and even set up sneaky defensive traps to deter other players and mobs!

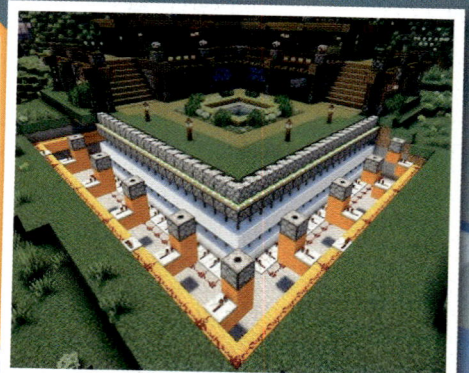

EXPLORING

You'll eventually need to wander further away from your base to find more resources. Over time you'll learn how to craft a map and compass – essential items for navigating.

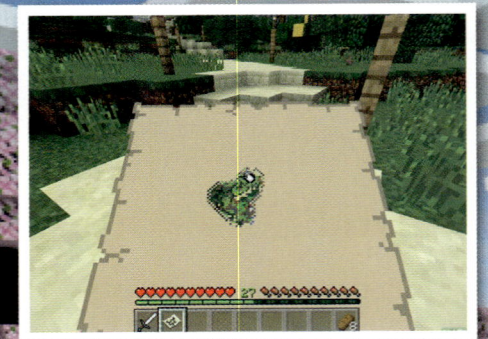

CHESTS

Players can only carry a certain number of items, so try to craft multiple chests on your journey. These storage spots can come in very handy as you begin to explore the Overworld.

TOOLS

You'll need to pack well for adventure and tools are essentials. Include some sort of spade, axe and pickaxe, especially when mining underground and harvesting resources.

WEAPONS AND ARMOUR

To protect yourself from mobs, ensure you have armour and a sword. Wooden versions are fine for starting out, but try to improve them over time by using tougher materials.

FOOD

You'll need something satisfying to eat after a hard day's mining, and tough battles will quickly deplete your energy levels, so be sure to take plenty of food supplies with you at all times.

COORDINATES

Minecraft players can use a special coordinates system to find their way around the Overworld. X measures longitude (west and east), Y measures altitude (north and south).

GOING UNDERGROUND

Eventually you'll need to head underground for even more resources and tougher adventures, with some truly rare blocks waiting to be found deep under the Overworld.

63

TEMPLES

Ancient temples can be found all over the Overworld, containing chests and traps. The structures can include desert and jungle pyramids, ocean monuments and woodland mansions.

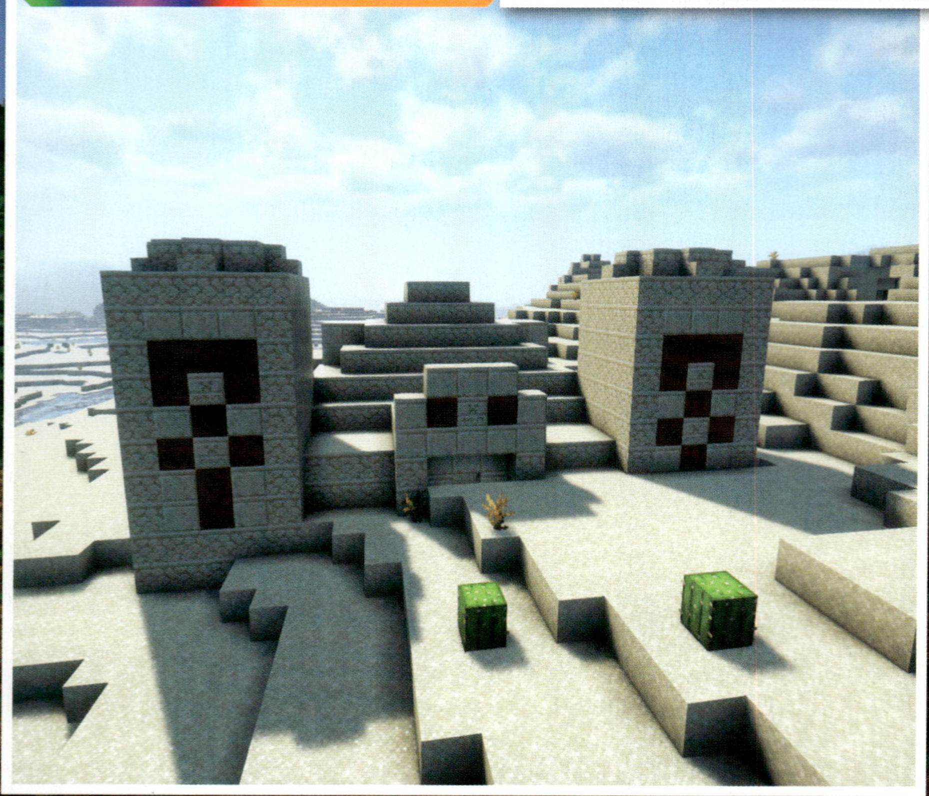

RECOVERY COMPASS

Players that die in the Overworld respawn somewhere else, but lose their inventory. To avoid that, be sure to craft a recovery compass and it'll guide you back to your loot.

ARCHAEOLOGY

Archaeology is a feature that allows players to use a crafted brush on suspicious sand and gravel blocks to unearth fossils and other historical artifacts such as pottery shards.

SMITHING

Take your crafting to the next level in the Overworld with a smithing table. Once obtained, players can use resources to upgrade their gear, add armour trims and smelt certain blocks.

SUNKEN SHIPS

When diving and exploring the ocean depths, players can come across shipwrecks. Although rare, these structures can often be home to treasure chests packed with precious loot.

VILLAGES

Whenever you find a village in the game, take the time to visit it. You'll be able to trade with wandering traders, encounter villagers, defend the locations from random raids and much more.

NETHER AND END PORTALS

Once you've spent enough time seeing what the Overworld has to offer, you might be ready for a new challenge. Turn to page 52 to find out how to access the Nether and page 70 for the End!

GAMESWARRIOR VERDICT

There's so much to see, do and experience in the Overworld that many players are still exploring these biomes years later. Take the time to discover everything the realm has to offer to become a true pro player!

GUIDE TO HOSTILE MOBS

All kids of mobs can be discovered during Minecraft travels – and some are downright hostile! GamesWarrior has collected all kinds of fun facts about these four mean mobs, and how players can successfully beat them when they encounter any in a battle!

MOB PROFILE: CREEPER

FACT-FILE

You're bound to bump into plenty of creepers during your adventures, but watch out, as they can silently approach you when you're not looking!

To defeat a creeper, hit them and then they'll start to flash and explode. Make sure you're standing far enough away from the blast though or you'll suffer damage too.

Defeated creepers can drop precious experience points, gunpowder, music discs and a creeper head that can be worn to scare your mates!

DAMAGE-ALERT!

If you encounter a creeper and don't have any armour yet, watch out. Unprotected players will be killed instantly by this mob's lethal blast!

A creeper that's been struck by lightning becomes a charged creeper. This effect amplifies its explosion power, making its blasts even more devastating.

STATS:
- SKILL: ★★★★☆
- STRENGTH: ★★★★★
- AGILITY: ★★★★★
- SPEED: ★★★★★
- COOLNESS: ★★★★★

OVERALL
★★★★☆

GAMESWARRIOR VERDICT
A silent but deadly mob!

MOB PROFILE: ZOMBIE

FACT-FILE

A shuffling undead mob, zombies have to be close to a player to cause damage, so they can always be pushed away or run away from.

Zombies are one of the most common hostile mobs in Minecraft. One on its own is simple enough to deal with, but it's easy to get overwhelmed by a large horde of them.

Basic zombies can be taken out with a sword swipe or arrows and drop rotten flesh. Watched out for much tougher armoured zombies with weapons though.

DAMAGE-ALERT!

Zombies that spawn during the day will burst into flames under the heat of the blazing sun, which makes them much easier to defeat!

There are actually many different variants of the standard zombie, including husks, drowned, zombie villagers, baby zombies and even chicken jockeys!

STATS:

- SKILL: ★★★★☆
- STRENGTH: ★★★★☆
- AGILITY: ★★★★☆
- SPEED: ★★★★☆
- COOLNESS: ★★★★★

OVERALL
★★★★☆

GAMESWARRIOR VERDICT

This undead mob can be an easy enemy to beat

67

MOB PROFILE: SKELETON

FACT-FILE

This undead mob can spawn in groups up to four skeletons at a time and they are usually armed with bows to target players from a distance.

Skeletons will always chase players they can see within 16 blocks, so try to stand your ground and fight them. You'll ideally need a shield and bow to ensure victory.

If you defeat a skeleton it will drop whatever equipment and weapons it was carrying, along with arrows, bones and a skeleton skull to wear!

DAMAGE-ALERT!

Try not to freak out the first time that you spot this spooky mob. Skeletons can always be beaten if you have some decent armour and weapons.

Variants of skeletons to watch out for include skeleton horsemen, strays in snowy biomes and bogged in swamp and mangrove swamp biomes.

STATS:
- SKILL: ★★★★☆
- STRENGTH: ★★★★★
- AGILITY: ★★★★★
- SPEED: ★★★★☆
- COOLNESS: ★★★★★

OVERALL
★★★★★

GAMESWARRIOR VERDICT
Watch out for this fast and lethal mob!

MOB PROFILE: ENDERMAN

FACT-FILE

Usually a neutral mob, endermen will attack players who damage them or look directly into their face. Just try to avoid doing either, if you can!

Endermen are the only mob that can spawn in all three dimensions, although players are much less likely to encounter them in the Overworld.

To effectively defeat an enderman, arm yourself with a diamond sword and good armour, hide out of sight, then attack it from behind before it can teleport away.

Defeat an enderman and it will drop a precious and rare ender pearl. This handy item can be thrown and instantly teleports the player to wherever it lands!

DAMAGE ALERT!

One of the fastest and toughest mobs to beat in Minecraft, endermen can dish out and take loads of punishment, so be warned if you see one.

STATS:

SKILL: ★★★★★
STRENGTH: ★★★★★
AGILITY: ★★★★★
SPEED: ★★★★★
COOLNESS: ★★★★★

OVERALL
★★★★★

GAMESWARRIOR VERDICT
Creepy, fast and deadly!

GUIDE TO THE END

Now that you're a pro Minecraft player, it's time to face the final challenge... the End! GamesWarrior has reviewed this dark, space-like dimension. It is home to the biggest mob in the game, the ender dragon, a tough foe that even the best gamers struggle to beat.

ENTER THE END

In order the reach the End, you'll need to construct an end portal. To do so, first find a stronghold using an eye of ender and then locate the portal room.

GAMESWARRIOR SAYS
Use the recipe below to craft a total of 12 eyes of ender, all of which you'll need to get the end portal working.

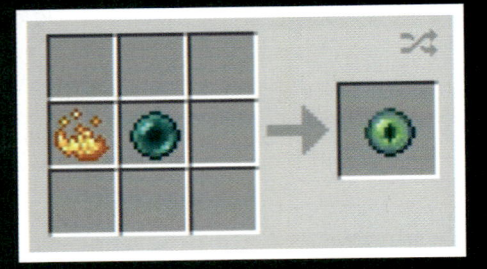

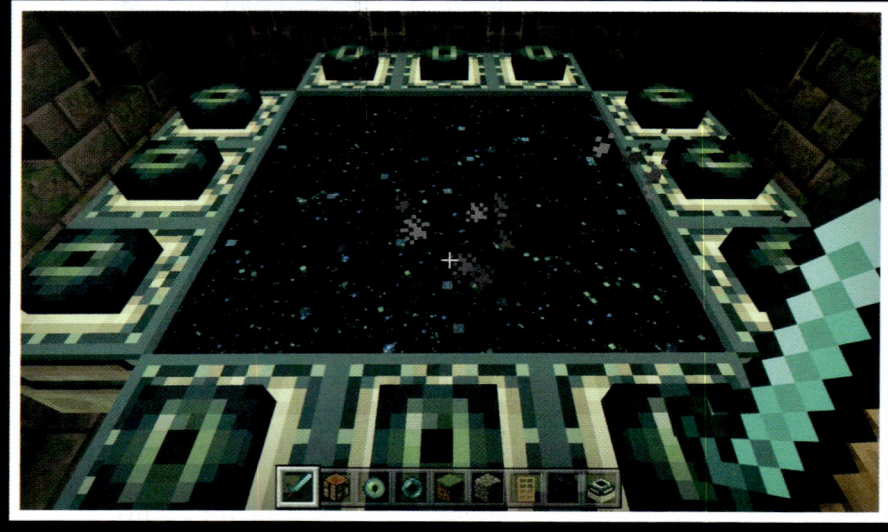

PORTAL ACTIVATION

Once you've managed to find the portal room within a stronghold, place the 12 eyes of ender into the slots around the frame to activate it and then step inside.

GAMESWARRIOR SAYS
Be sure to stand back once the end portal starts up, as the area around is destroyed with a powerful explosion!

END ENVIRONMENT

Stepping into the End reveals a single large island surrounded by lots of smaller islands. There's no daylight cycle or weather in the dimension, just a constant dim light.

GAMESWARRIOR SAYS
Be careful to avoid falling off the edge of any of the islands in the End, otherwise you'll fall into the void below!

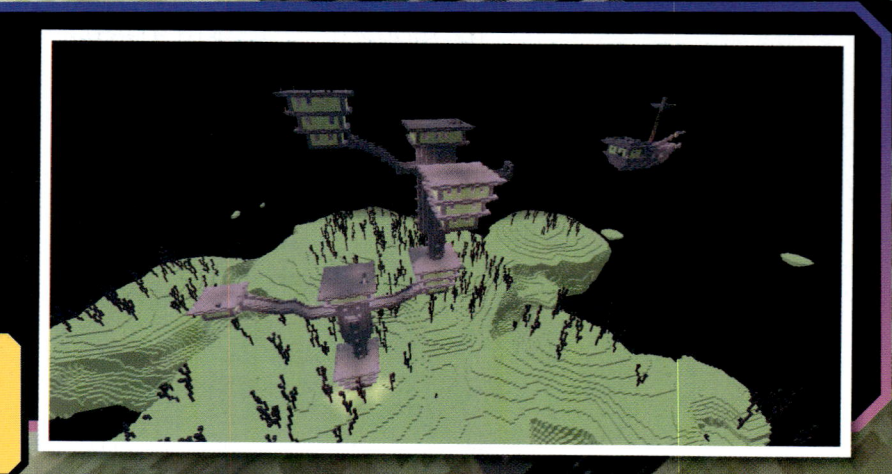

END STONE

Almost everything in the End is constructed from end stone, a tough block that can be mined and has three times more blast resistance than ordinary stone.

GAMESWARRIOR SAYS

End stone is a very handy block, as it can't be moved by endermen or destroyed by the ender dragon.

END BLOCKS

Blocks that can only be found in the End include end stone, chorus flower, chorus plant, purpur blocks, end gateway, end portal, end crystal and dragon egg.

GAMESWARRIOR SAYS

Mining any of the items above means you can take them back to the Overworld with you... if you survive the ender dragon that is!

END STRUCTURES

In addition to floating islands, visitors to the End can expect to find end cities, end ships, chorus trees, end gateway portals and the exit portal.

GAMESWARRIOR SAYS

Be sure to take your time exploring all that the End has to offer, as there are kinds of useful items to pick up.

EXPLODING BEDS

Some items in your inventory may act very strangely in the End, such as compasses not working, clocks spinning wildly and beds exploding.

GAMESWARRIOR SAYS

One advantage to being in the End is that fire will burn indefinitely when placed on bedrock blocks, which can come in very handy.

END MOBS

Only three mobs exist in the End – endermen, shulkers and the ender dragon. Each is tough to beat, so tread carefully when battling them.

GAMESWARRIOR SAYS

Shulkers spawn in end cities and attack by firing homing bullets that cause Levitation, making players float upward.

BATTLE REWARDS

Brave players who do manage to defeat the ender dragon will be rewarded with 12,000 experience points and a rare dragon egg.

GAMESWARRIOR SAYS

It's possible to resummon the ender dragon by placing four end crystals on the edges of the exit portal to make the mob respawn.

ENDER DRAGON

The ender dragon guards the end gateways, the only way back to the Overworld. The mob flies around the area and will attack players who get to near!

GAMESWARRIOR SAYS

Watch out for the ender dragon's fireballs; lethal blasts that deal plenty of magic damage and can't be deflected.

RETURN TO THE OVERWORLD

Once the ender dragon has been beaten, the exit portal will activate and allow players to step inside and be transported back to the Overworld.

GAMESWARRIOR SAYS

Don't forget to make sure you pick up any and all items that you may need in the End before stepping into the portal!

MOB PROFILE: ENDER DRAGON

FACT FILE

The most powerful mob in Minecraft, the ender dragon is a hostile flying creature that guards access to the end gateways.

Before battling the mob, arm yourself with a diamond or netherite sword and armour, an enchanted bow and lots of food and healing potions!

Taking out the end crystals on top of each obsidian pillar then allows players to attack the ender dragon directly.

You can always use your bow or a crossbow to attack the mob from a distance, but watch out for its deadly fireball attacks.

DAMAGE ALERT!

Multiple attempts may be required to ultimately defeat the ender dragon, but the unique rewards make it well worth it!

STATS:
- SKILL: ★★★★★
- STRENGTH: ★★★★★
- AGILITY: ★★★★☆
- SPEED: ★★★★★
- COOLNESS: ★★★★★

OVERALL ★★★★★

GAMESWARRIOR VERDICT
The ultimate Minecraft mob and challenge!

See how many of these words you can find in the grid below. We've highlighted one to get you started!

```
R E K L U H S M T O U B K W D E
U E B D N E N D C R Y S T A L N
I N I R E D N E F O E Y E E L O
P D B U F E N D S T O N E W A G
O P U T F R W I C B S O N U B A
J O B S I D I A N I R E D B E R
D R A G O N E G G B T J S F R D
G T H E V O I D J E W Y H O I R
J A Y T R O I G Y R E H I R F E
K L O E C P U T Y W R E P B J D
O C H O R U S F L O W E R U Y N
J T P U R P U R B L O C K B J E
```

- ✓ END CITY
- ☐ END STONE
- ☐ END PORTAL
- ☐ DRAGON EGG
- ☐ END SHIP
- ☐ PURPUR BLOCK
- ☐ END CRYSTAL
- ☐ CHORUS FLOWER
- ☐ SHULKER
- ☐ FIREBALL
- ☐ OBSIDIAN
- ☐ EYE OF ENDER
- ☐ THE VOID
- ☐ ENDER DRAGON

MEGA MINECRAFT QUIZ

Do you think you're a massive Minecraft fan? If so, it's time to find out how much you really know about one of the biggest video games in the world! Take the GamesWarrior Mega Minecraft quiz and discover if you're an Overworld noob or a Mojang legend, with a score that matches your knowledge.

1 In what year was Minecraft created?

2 How many default skins are currently available in Minecraft?

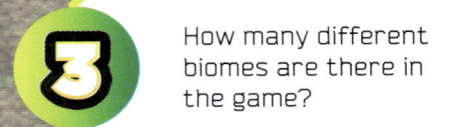

3 How many different biomes are there in the game?

4 What new mob was introduced in the pale garden biome?

5 In which biome can you find skulk blocks?

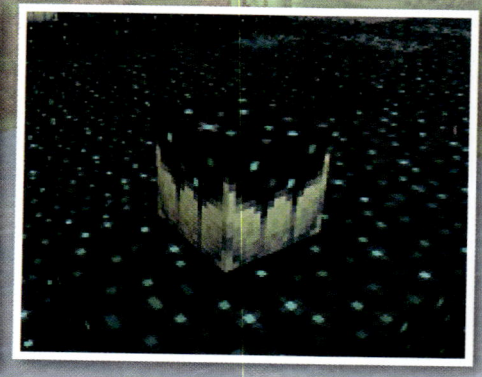

6 At what event did Mojang reveal the Spring to Life update?

7 Which aquatic Minecraft build was created by Junghan Kim (Owlhouse)?

8 What kind of map do you need to find trial chambers?

9 What year was *A Minecraft Movie* released?

10 What's the last block you need to place in order to spawn a wither?

11 Which mob bursts into flames in sunshine?

12 What is the final mob in the End?

13 What year were horses added to Minecraft?

14 Where in the game can players buy skin packs?

15 Which block should you break to defeat a creaking?

16 How many different kinds of frog are there in Minecraft?

17 What structures naturally occur in the deep dark?

GAMESWARRIOR SAYS
All of the answers to the Mega Minecraft quiz can be found in this guide!

18 How many obsidian blocks are required to make a nether portal?

19 Which actor stars as Steve in *A Minecraft Movie*?

20 How much did Microsoft manage to buy Mojang for in 2014?

21 In which Minecraft biomes do beds always explode?

22 When was the first-ever Minecraft novel released?

23 Which mob comes in handy for repelling creepers and phantoms?

24 What year did Minecraft celebrate its 15th anniversary?

25 How many main game modes are there in Minecraft?

26 How many Caves & Cliffs updates were released for Minecraft in 2021?

27 Which blind mob spawns in the deep dark?

28 Purpur blocks can only be found in which biome?

29 Some fans were very excited when which mob appeared in *A Minecraft Movie*?

30 What was the only playable mob available when Minecraft launched?

31 Which precious item can be used to barter with piglins?

32 How many minutes does the Hero of the Village status effect last for?

33 What does a creeper tranforms into if struck by lightning?

34 Which part of an enderman should you not stare at for too long?

35 What year was Minecraft Dungeons released?

36 What's the name of the rare cow variant?

37 How many experience points do players receive for beating the ender dragon?

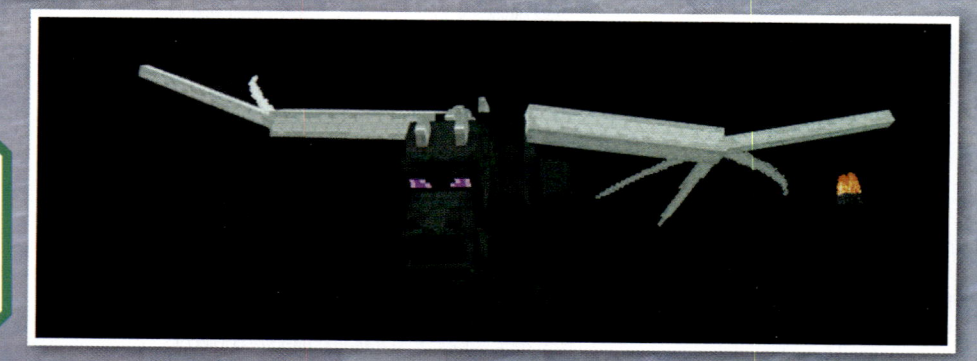

38 Which block is created when water flows over lava?

39 In which UK city can fans enjoy the Minecraft Experience: Villager Rescue?

40 When was Minecraft Earth officially shut down?

QUIZ ANSWERS

1	2009	19	Jack Black	30	Steve
2	Nine	20	$2.5 billion	31	Gold ingots
3	60	21	The Nether	32	40
4	Creaking	22	2017	33	A charged creeper
5	The deep dark	23	Cats	34	Face
6	Minecraft Live 2025	24	2024	35	2020
7	Sea Diary	25	Four	36	Mooshroom
8	Trial explorer map	26	Two	37	12,000
9	2025	27	The warden	38	Obsidian
10	Wither skeleton skull	28	The End	39	London
11	Zombie	29	Chicken jockey	40	2021
12	Ender dragon				
13	2013				
14	Minecraft Marketplace				
15	Creaking heart				
16	Three				
17	Ancient cities				
18	14				

GAMESWARRIOR VERDICT

1-15: Great start! Keep exploring the Overworld to learn more.

16-25: Very impressive. You definitely know plenty about Minecraft!

26-40: Wow, what an amazing score. You're a Minecraft master!

PAGE 21 - CREAKING

There are six Creaking in the picture.

PAGE 33 - CODE BREAKER

STEALTH, AVOID, SNEAK, QUIETLY, SLOWLY, SECRETLY, DODGE, SIDESTEP, CAREFULLY, SILENT

PAGE 45 - TRIAL CHAMBER MAZE

PAGE 59 - TRADING TANGLE

Bell, Golden Apple, Explorer Map, Lapus Lazuli Ore, Coral Block

PAGE 51 - ENCHANTMENT EXPERT

Feather Falling – Diamond armour

Fire Aspect – Sword

Silk Touch – Shovel

Luck of the Sea – Fishing rod

Impaling – Trident

PAGE 73 - ENDER WORDSEARCH

77

GAMESWARRIOR
EXPERT REVIEWS BY EXPERT GAMERS

LET'S TALK GAMESWARRIOR
LEVEL UP WITH OUR ULTIMATE GAMING GUIDES, 2026 EDITIONS AND ADVENT CALENDAR!

GW'S ULTIMATE UNOFFICIAL GAMING GUIDES

With insights from the experts at GamesWarrior, our Ultimate Gaming Guides review the biggest gaming brands and give their expert views and opinions on everything from enhancing strategies to becoming a true pro!

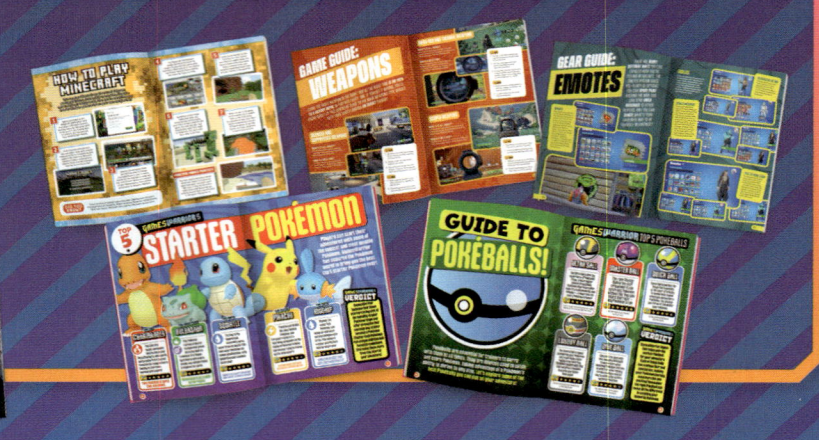

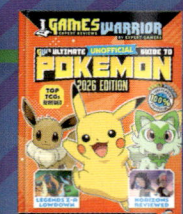

GW'S ULTIMATE UNOFFICIAL 2026 EDITIONS

Whether you're a seasoned expert or dropping in for the first time GamesWarrior's 2026 Editions have everything you need to know about the most successful gaming franchises in the world!

These make ideal Christmas presents for die-hard fans!

GW'S ULTIMATE UNOFFICIAL ADVENT CALENDAR

Get ready for Christmas with the experts at GamesWarrior!

Behind each of the 24 doors, you'll find a mini book filled with expert reviews on gaming strategies, brilliant builds and much more!

The perfect build up to the BIG DAY for all fans!

Full range available at amazon.co.uk and other good book retailers.

www.littlebrotherbooks.co.uk

Little Brother Books Limited, Ground Floor, 23 Southernhay East, Exeter, Devon, EX1 1QL

All covers are subject to change. ©2025 Little Brother Books Ltd.

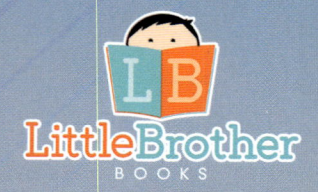

Little Brother BOOKS